The
Journey

Christian Spiritual Formation
in the Life of a Small Group

Barb Nardi Kurtz

DISCIPLESHIP RESOURCES

P.O. BOX 340003 • NASHVILLE, TN 37203-0003
www.discipleshipresources.org

Cover and book design by Joey McNair

Edited by Debra D. Smith and David Whitworth

ISBN 0-88177-326-3

Library of Congress Catalog Card No. 00-105448

DR326

Table of Contents

Acknowledgments

My faith has been nurtured by the people of Laurel Heights United Methodist Church in San Antonio, Texas, for many years. Some of the people there are cherished friends. Some of them have participated in the writing of this book. Many colleagues in ministry in other places have shared their thoughts and practice for these pages. I give thanks for them all.

To all those who have shared their stories; to Tammy and Melissa and Jeff, who read and critiqued the manuscript; and especially to the Viva Monday Morning Reunion, my deepest thanks. You have blessed me!

I am most grateful for Tom, companion on my own heart's journey. The loving relationship in which our faith has been shaped over the last five years is God's incredible gift.

Barb Nardi Kurtz

Chapter One
Introduction

For I give water in the wilderness,
   rivers in the desert,
to give drink to my chosen people,
   the people whom I formed for myself
so that they might declare my praise.
                              Isaiah 43:20-21

A tale from Jewish folklore teaches that we are created deep in the heart of God, who whispers to us all the secrets of creation before we are born. We rest in God and experience the depth and extent of God's love for us. In the pain and shock of birth, we forget. Our whole lives thereafter are a journey back toward our first home in God—a time and place we only dimly and occasionally recall.

As I have experienced my own Christian journey and accompanied others on their paths, I have come to understand this story as a metaphor for the human quest for meaning, for relationship with the power we sense beyond ourselves. Humans—religious and otherwise—spend our lives trying to make sense of our existence. That search may take the form of seeking material wealth or excitement and adventure or fame. We may work to excel at teaching or mentoring the young or otherwise making some lasting contribution to society. Christians believe the meaning we all seek is found in relationship to God through Jesus Christ. As Saint Augustine once wrote, "Thou hast formed us for thyself, and our hearts are restless 'till they find rest in thee."

Over the centuries of Christian faith, communities have formed patterns of seeking God through Christ. In the highly individualistic modern Western culture, many people make this quest for meaning independently. Although I grew up in and was shaped in the church, for some time as an adult I was one of those searching for the rich and full reality of God's love "on my own."

As a burned-out church professional several years ago I was given the opportunity to become part of a covenant prayer group. In the small community of that group, we all learned to listen for God. Together, we made space and time in our lives for the habits that prepared us to recognize the loving and gracious presence of God with us. We studied Scripture and other sacred writings and prayed for one another and the world. We fasted and talked about the change in focus we experienced during the fast. We attended worship in our various congregations regularly and shared our reflections on that worship. We encouraged one another to partake of Holy Communion whenever it was available, and together we recalled and reflected upon our baptism and its meaning. We talked about our growing faith and held one another accountable for the ways we lived out that faith.

We became part of one another's lives in ways none of us had previously experienced. We were present to one another through the birth of grandchildren and problems with teenage sons and daughters. We prayed for one another through one spouse's job search and another's career change. When my own husband was dying and I could not even pray, my covenant friends prayed through that time for me. Four years later when I met the man who is now my spouse the covenant group celebrated God's gift of a new relationship.

The Grace-Filled Journey

Through the years of our covenant relationship we came to know God—the grace, mercy, and love of God—present in our lives. We were all changed. That process of change is called spiritual formation. It is a grace-filled journey that continues as long as we live. It begins when we first recognize that knowing God in Jesus Christ is our goal. It is the subject of this book.

Each one of us is a unique, mysterious whole—body, mind, and spirit. There is in each of us a deep center wherein dwell our greatest hopes and dreams and fears, our visions of the future, and our sacred memories. This center is our spirit. It is in the spirit that God is present in each of God's children. It is the spirit that drives—motivates and inspires—mind and body.

So much has been written about life in the spirit and spiritual formation in the last several years that it is possible to find a definition and a theory to fit almost any secular or religious view. There are those who talk about spiritual formation as realization of the highest self, without defining either *realization* or *highest self.* There are some who will say that spiritual wholeness comes in knowing and accepting one's self without qualification—and without reference to God. Some go so far as to believe they can become their own god. There is no need, in the minds of these practitioners, for our "spirituality" to make any difference in the way we relate to the world around us.

There are many who believe that the way to success in any business or professional endeavor is a well-developed spiritual life—with or without relationship to any higher power. Businesses hire consultants to take leaders on spiritual life retreats to discover "their best selves" in a process of self-exploration. Looking under *spiritual life* on the Internet, I found "Tarot," "Astrology," "New Age," and a host of other headings. It seemed to me like one more list of ways to spend recreation time. Included in that list was an entry for *religion*, as well as one for *spiritual formation*.

Christian Spiritual Life

When Christians talk about spiritual life and the process of spiritual formation we are not discussing recreation, though recreation and play are an important part of life. We are talking about the very heart of life. For Christians, the spiritual life is perhaps best described as the journey of discovering our own inner selves and the God who waits there for us. As we come to know ourselves, and God, we can grow into the image and likeness of God in which the creation stories of Genesis tell us we were all made.

For the Christian, spiritual life is not simply spending half an hour in the morning or evening in prayer. Spiritual life is *all* of life, lived in relationship to God through Jesus Christ. The spiritual life—Christian formation—is not our work alone. God plays the major role. In baptism, God claims us. Our sins forgiven, our lives redeemed, we obtain the possibility of life lived in relationship to God through Jesus Christ. We have only to be open to God. That life in God is a promise made to us by Jesus when he said, "I came that [you] may have life, and have it abundantly" (John 10:10). We can trust that promise and seek to find its fulfillment. In our experience of the church, we can begin to learn how to live as people who have been promised abundant life.

When I was growing up in Redwood City, California, our family attended First Methodist Episcopal Church. My husband, Tom, and I went back to see that church recently. The warm red-brick building was not as large as I thought it would be. I remembered it as huge, with heavy wooden front doors and great stained-glass windows. There would be glowing wood and brick inside, long halls, a cavernous fellowship hall, and a wide, shallow auditorium with walls that slid back when we had large crowds. Other than size, the church still looks much the same inside and out, still surrounded by its colorful garden. The building is in a changing neighborhood, and serves both Korean and English-speaking congregations.

I remember potluck suppers in the fellowship hall of that church when I was very young. We ate mountains of mashed potatoes and fried chicken and artichokes from my uncle Charley's garden. I remember Sunday school classes with gentle-voiced teachers who told us the stories of Jesus and sent us home with beautiful picture story cards. I remember Saturday mornings.

Each Saturday morning the Altar Guild dusted and polished the sanctuary furniture and arranged the altar flowers for worship. For the first ten years of my life I was part of this ritual with my mother and her friends. We began by praying together in the big old kitchen, asking God to bless our work. Then we gathered clean cloths and lemon oil, gladiolas or dahlias or sweet peas brought from home gardens, and shears and containers and headed off to ready the sanctuary for Sunday worship. I got to carry a dust cloth and, with my friends Pat and Adele, to polish sections of the communion rail. We were always careful in our work; for we knew what we did was an offering to God. God's house was a place where we were welcome and trusted. Who we were and what we did was valued and appreciated.

I belonged in that church family before I understood what the word meant. That experience of belonging, of contributing to the ministry of the congregation, even before I could read or cross the street alone, began the process of my Christian formation. In the community of that Methodist church, I was introduced to the means of grace. I was being shaped in ways John Wesley advocated and wrote about two hundred years ago.

Wesley, the Means of Grace, and Formation

Many modern United Methodists believe that there is no tradition of spiritual formation in our denomination. In reality, we have a rich tradition of spiritual formation. John Wesley's approach to Christian spiritual formation was unique. Through the experiences of his own life journey, Wesley came to understand that our relationship with God begins with self-knowledge and repentance. He believed that by participating in the means of grace we experience the holiness of God, we are convinced of the depth of our own sin and separation, and we repent—that is, turn our lives in a new direction. Repentance leads to the transformed heart and the transformed life. We can begin to accept the forgiveness God offers. We learn to trust in the love of God in Jesus Christ and respond to that love and grace by loving God in return. Our love for God is shown in our concern for the poor and suffering in our world, and we are led to acts of mercy in Christ's name. In loving relationship with

God and service to others we find true joy. As part of a congregation in Redwood City I was beginning, as a young child, to experience the holiness of God and the joy of praising and serving God.

Wesley taught that the means of grace are essential to the process of formation. Means of grace are habits and practices that become channels through which we experience God's grace. Wesley divided these disciplines into two general categories, works of mercy and works of piety.

Works of mercy are service to others in Christ's name. Wesley clearly understood that as we serve others, particularly those most neglected by society at large, we experience God. In acts of mercy we take seriously Jesus' statement that "just as you did it to one of the least of these who are members of my family, you did it to me" (Matthew 25:40). When we have a relationship with the "least of these" we have a relationship with Jesus. In today's language we sometimes refer to acts of mercy as acts of justice and acts of compassion.

The other category is works of piety. In today's usage the word *piety* sometimes has negative connotations and may be taken to mean an overzealous religiosity. For Wesley, *piety* simply meant actively seeking a relationship with God. The terms *acts of worship* and *acts of devotion* are helpful in understanding works of piety. Works of piety can be thought of as essential spiritual disciplines for growing as disciples. Works of piety include corporate and personal worship, prayer, fasting, Holy Communion, Bible study, and Christian conferencing. Just as works of mercy are channels through which we meet God, works of piety are also channels through which God works in our lives.

Salvation comes only by God's grace, through faith, not through engaging in a certain set of practices. For the Christian, faith is a relationship to God through Jesus Christ. The daily practice of the means of grace is the way this relationship is nurtured, the way the spiritual lives of Christians are formed. Building a relationship with God must be a way of life, part of the fabric of every day's activity.

Growing in Faith

We all come to faith in different ways. We grow in faith in different ways. Our personalities, our cultures, our other life experiences are all in play in our developing relationship with God.

Some of us are born into the church, baptized and claimed as infants, gradually growing into faith as we grow in years. Our coming to know God is a slow, at times imperceptible movement. Some of us encounter God in a single, striking moment of conversion. Faith is then informed and nourished in the life of a congregation. Some of us come to faith as we find God in service to others. Our faith is nourished by prayer and by the companionship of others within the community of believers.

Each of us has a relationship to God that is as unique as we ourselves are. There are many means of grace, ways in which we experience God's grace. Each of us builds a life of faith using differing combinations of these life-giving activities. We do not shape ourselves; that is God's doing. It is the means of grace which open us to God's working in us.

Sanctification is the process of being formed as Christian disciples. This process of formation, or sanctification, is different for every person. But however we come to Christ, the process of sanctification, Christian formation, is a gradual, step-by-step affair. It is a lifelong journey of the heart empowered by the Holy Spirit and informed by the Scriptures, by our long Christian tradition, and by participation in Christian community.

Wesley knew that one cannot become a disciple, be formed in the image of God, alone. He organized Methodists of his day into small groups called classes, where they shared their growing faith. They were held accountable for practicing works of piety in their daily lives and living out their faith in works of mercy.

Like one of the early Methodist classes, my covenant group practiced these means of grace and our relationship to God flourished. We learned from our own experience that becoming fully Christian is not something one does on one's own. Whether working, studying, worshiping, or playing together, Christians support one another in the quest to grow in the image of God. One's Christian friends can be voices for God in one's life, mirrors of one's belief and behavior. Friends can hold each other accountable for the ways in which they live out their faith in the real world. Becoming a disciple of Jesus Christ does not happen in a vacuum!

Formation and the Local Church

The logical place for Christian formation to happen is in the local church. Just as spiritual life is central to the life of the Christian disciple, so spiritual life and spiritual formation are central to the life of the church, the body of Christ. There are many small groups formed exclusively for spiritual formation, but every small group in the congregation can—and should—be a place where formation takes place.

Several years ago, the congregation where I worship formed a task force to help the congregation discern their path for corporate ministry in the future.

Members of that small group spent time in prayer and fasting and searching the Scriptures over the period of a year. It was a formational experience for all of them. In the congregational meeting at the end of the discernment process Wendell Davis, one of the task group members, told us that being part of the disciplined group had changed his life. "My faith has grown because of my participation in this process, and I will never be the same," he said.

Congregational life is the sum of all the activities of the congregation's members. In that life we have great opportunity to help our members become open to God's shaping power. Every small group in the life of the congregation can be a place of Christian formation. The remainder of this book will be taken up with ways we can make all the small groups of a congregation places where members can engage in Christian formation. Whether it is in serving groups, learning groups, administering groups, groups for accountability, or groups designed for support or fellowship, every member of every group in your congregation can participate in the means of grace. Every member of every group can come to know who and whose they are through the shaping power of God.

Jeff's Story

A case in point is the story of my friend Jeff, whose faith has deepened greatly in the five years I have known him. Jeff's lively relationship to God is reflected in his concern for other people, his active prayer life, his participation in the life of the congregation, and his attitude of joy.

When he came to San Antonio, Jeff had been away from the church for fifteen years. Raised in an active and loving congregation, considering seminary and full-time ministry when he graduated from college, Jeff had discovered conflicts in his understanding of faith that sent him out of the church for what he calls "a time in the wilderness."

Jeff's wilderness time ended when he got lost one day and came across Laurel Heights United Methodist Church as he stopped at an intersection. God has been at work in Jeff during his time at Laurel Heights in the life of the small groups of which he has been a part. In a DISCIPLE Bible study group Jeff learned to search the Scriptures not only for knowledge and understanding but for illumination in daily challenges and problems as well. In his Sunday school class he had weekly conversation with others who were seeking relationship with God. In an Emmaus reunion group he was held accountable for his pattern of discipleship and performed that same service for others. As part of a Habitat for Humanity team, he worked to help families create secure homes and reflected on that work. Working with the Senior High

Youth Fellowship, Jeff developed—and encouraged in the group by his example—the habit of praying daily for all the youth and their leaders. The youth group members have seen one another through some harrowing times in the years Jeff has worked with them, and they have prayed for each other every step of the way.

In corporate worship, he had access to Holy Communion and the read and preached Word. In all these settings God was at work through the means of grace, and Jeff was being formed into the person he is today. Participation in the small-group life of the congregation—for learning, for service, for accountability—has been a pivotal element in Jeff's journey. His journey is not complete. There have been changes in Jeff's life situation in the past two years, and there are changes yet to come as he pursues a major career change at midlife. Through all these changes Jeff has found personal peace, trust of God's loving will for him, and a sense of abiding joy that brings to life Paul's words to his friends in Philippi: "My brothers and sisters, rejoice in the Lord" (Philippians 3:1).

Every Group a Place of Formation

Formation does not happen automatically just because a group is meeting in the church or meeting to carry out church business. Making every group in your congregation a place of spiritual formation will require effort and determination. Participating with one another in the means of grace can provide support for formation in any group in any congregation.

Three key elements can contribute to making small groups that already exist in the life of your church into places of Christian formation. The first is lay leaders prepared for formational leadership and willing to spend time and energy preparing for each meeting and communicating with members. The second is a meeting plan centered in one or more of the means of grace—prayer, searching the Scripture, fasting, corporate worship including the sacraments, and Christian conferencing. The third and critical element is prayer by staff and lay leadership on a consistent and long-term basis.

Supported by continuing prayer, led by equipped and willing people, and focusing on one or more of the means of grace, every small group in your congregation can contribute to the positive Christian formation of its members, creating a congregation of committed and joyful disciples of Jesus Christ.

A congregation of disciples, able to rejoice in the Lord and serving the world in Christ's name, can transform the community around it.

All human beings seek to find meaning in their lives. For the Christian, meaning comes in relationship to God through Jesus Christ. This seeking can take many forms or patterns.

- The church talks about this seeking after God as Christian spiritual formation.
- The process of spiritual formation is not work that we can do ourselves, it is God's working in us.
- There are patterns of discipline that can make us open to God and God's shaping work. These channels through which we experience God are means of grace.

All of us have memories of the events that have shaped us as human beings, whether Christian or not.

- What are the events that have shaped you positively as a Christian?
- Do you remember instances in which you were shaped in a negative way? Let yourself be open to God in prayer for healing of those instances.
- As you read this book, look for ways that your life can be made even more open to God's shaping power.

Chapter Two
Means of Grace

For it is God who is at work in you, enabling you both to will and to work for his good pleasure.

Philippians 2:13

Valli poured water from a clear glass pitcher into the baptismal shell as John read the Thanksgiving Over the Water from the baptismal liturgy. The only sounds in the church were the pouring water and John's voice. Then John took Logan, age four months, in his arms and baptized him "in the name of the Father and of the Son and of the Holy Spirit" as the congregation stood watching. His parents and the two pastors laid hands on his head to bless him, and Logan was carried into the congregation. "Logan, child of God, meet your new family of faith," John said. After worship, friends and family continued to celebrate this great day in Logan's young life.

What was happening here? In the midst of worship on this bright Sunday morning, Logan was claimed as a member of the family of God. Baptism is the sacrament of entry into the church. It is one of the two sacramental ways in which God draws close and offers God's self to us. In baptism, the gift comes through water and the laying on of hands. In the Lord's Supper, which is also called Eucharist or Holy Communion, the vehicle is the bread and cup. These holy moments are common to the worship life of your congregation. They are at once obvious and yet mysterious ways in which God intersects with our lives.

Baptism and Holy Communion are most often celebrated in the gathered worshiping community. In the United Methodist tradition these sacraments are administered by ordained clergy (or those appointed to a particular charge under the supervision of a district superintendent). We understand both sacraments to be "means of grace by which God works invisibly in us, quickening, strengthening, and confirming our faith" (from *The Book of Discipline of The United Methodist Church—2000*. Copyright © 2000 by The United Methodist Publishing House; ¶ 103, p. 68. Used by permission.).

Other means of grace are both public and private and are not considered sacraments. They are equally important, however, and there is a sense in which each of them is sacred. In the previous chapter means of grace were described in terms of works of mercy and works of piety. Nonsacramental means of grace include worship, prayer, Bible study, fasting, service to others, and Christian conferencing. Each of them brings us closer to God. It is through the continuing practice of the means of grace that we are formed as Christian disciples.

In this book we will be examining how various means of grace can be incorporated into the ongoing life of every small group, so that all small groups in the church become places where disciples are formed and nurtured. Before looking at the specific role of the means of grace in the small group we will review the general role of several means of grace.

Prayer

Nothing can substitute for prayer in the devotional life. It is our means of communication with the One who created us.

We pray because it is our primary connection with God—both talking to God and listening for God. We pray to give thanks for the gifts of life and the blessings of each day. We pray to praise the Creator. We pray for guidance, for healing, for forgiveness, for grace. We intercede for others and pray in supplication for ourselves.

Prayer changes us. The psalmist wrote, "While I kept silence, my body wasted away through my groaning all day long. . . . Then I acknowledged my sin to you, and I did not hide my iniquity; . . . and you forgave the guilt of my sin" (Psalm 32:3, 5).

As we pray, offering our guilt and pain and our joys and celebrations to God, we learn to trust in the One who hears our prayers, so that with the psalmist we can say, "I rejoice in the LORD" (Psalm 104:34).

How We Pray

Prayer can happen both privately and corporately—at home, in meetings and social gatherings, and in worship. We pray silently and aloud, in writing and through music and the other arts. Private prayer is essential to devotional life. Corporate prayer is important as well because it reminds us that we are all a part of the community of faith, the body of Christ. Corporate prayer can be spoken by the group, using the common, historic prayers of the church. It can also be silent, as in confession or intercession.

Private prayer is different for each person. There are many "authorities" who write and speak about prayer, but no one individual can tell another the "right" way to pray. Prayer is between the individual and God, and what is right for you is what brings you closer to God. If you are new to the daily practice of prayer, you might want to use the classic prayers of your tradition at first, reading them aloud or silently. You might pray the Psalms or portions of the Gospels. Perhaps there is an order for morning or evening prayer available to use. You might pray your own prayers aloud, or silently, or write them in a journal.

The variety of ways to pray is almost endless. Whether we pray silently, in writing, or aloud, extemporaneously or using the written prayers of others, our prayers will most likely include adoration, confession, thanksgiving, and intercession or supplication. Adoration is our acknowledgement of who God is in our lives, our statement of allegiance and praise. In confession, we acknowledge who we are and ask forgiveness and grace. Our thanksgiving is not only for God's mercy and grace but also for all the other gifts of our lives. Supplication and intercession lead us outside ourselves to offer the joys and challenges of others to God. Our prayer will also include listening. In all our prayer, we need to leave time and space to listen for the One to whom we have been speaking.

Pray in the morning and/or in the evening. Pray all day—whenever you make a phone call, read or answer a letter, or go to an appointment, pray for the person whom you will contact. When any group gathering begins, pray for the participants. When any person comes to mind during the day, pray for that person. When you undertake any task, small or great, ask God's guidance. Pray, as Paul urges us, without ceasing! Keep prayer at the center of your life, and you will know God is there.

Searching the Scriptures

The Bible is the witness to God's continuing relationship with humankind. It can form and inform our spiritual lives. Generally we study Scripture to learn about it. We seek to know the audience for whom a book was written, the conditions in which it came into being, its meaning for the time in which it was written. We try to learn the setting in which a story took place or in which the prophet wrote so that we might better understand what we are reading. Bible study is the way to better understand what we believe.

Searching the Scriptures is reading the Bible in order to hear what God is saying to our lives today, to hear the guidance there for us, to find inspiration for our own lives of faith. When we search the Scripture alone or as part of a group, we ask a different sort of questions. We may ask, "What does this passage say to me about God and the relationship between God and God's people?" or "How is God speaking to me through this passage?" We might ask, "What is God asking of me here?" or "What is God offering to me?" or even "Who am I or where am I in this story?"

The questions we ask as we search the Scriptures will enrich and deepen our relationship to God. They will also help us to be aware of where that relationship is leading us. A daily pattern of reading Scripture is one way to claim this holy habit. You might want to follow the lectionary in any of the devotional guides available through your denomination. There are many individual devotional Bible series available in Christian bookstores.

Another way of searching the Scripture is the prayer form called sacred reading. The Latin term for this ancient practice is *lectio divina*. Sacred reading is simply reading Scripture through several times in a prayerful attitude with meditation and contemplation. This can be done alone or with a group. At the first reading, just enjoy the passage, reading it like a loving letter from a friend. At the second reading, imagine yourself in the story. What are the sights and sounds of the people and place in the passage? Let yourself feel the story as a participant. Think a few moments about what you have read. At the third reading, go slowly, savoring the words again, and listening for God's word to you in the words. Spend a few moments in silence thinking about what God has said to you through this passage. End your reading with a prayer of thanksgiving and perhaps writing in a journal about this experience of searching Scripture.

Keeping the Fast

Fasting is unfamiliar to many modern Protestant Christians, though it is mentioned in both Old and New Testament Scriptures. Fasting is most widely understood as abstaining from food. It can also be seen as abstaining for a period of time from a particular activity in order to focus more clearly on God. For example, if you are seeking to discern where God is leading you in your work life, you may want to "fast" from recreational reading or television for a week, in order to focus energy on searching the Scripture and prayer.

Your first fast might be from conversation, so that you spend a day in silent reflection. You may decide to fast from shopping! Perhaps you may choose the traditional fast from food. If you have never tried fasting from food, you may want to begin with a six- or eight-hour fast from after breakfast to dinnertime. A second time you might want to progress to a longer fast, whether twenty-four, thirty, or thirty-six hours.

You might fast as part of a Holy Week observation or as an act of worship at any time. Here are a few hints to help you get started. Always eat a light meal before you begin a fast—fruit and cereal and milk at breakfast, or a salad and fruit at lunch or dinnertime. During your fast, you may have herbal tea to drink, as well as plenty of water or clear fruit juice like apple or cranberry. Don't take tea or coffee or other stimulants during the fast. Break your fast with another light meal with fresh fruit or vegetables and cereal grains. It is a good idea to eat lightly of meat protein before and right after your fast. When you fast from food, don't try a fast longer than thirty-six hours without talking with your physician.

Try to set a goal for your fast so that it is a purposeful activity. For instance, you may want to fast in observance of world hunger, giving the money you would have spent on food in that time to hunger relief. Spend your ordinary meal time in prayer for those who work to end world hunger or studying ways you can work to ease the plight of the hungry in your community.

However you decide to fast, it is well to remember this advice from Jesus: "And whenever you fast, do not look dismal, like the hypocrites, for they disfigure their faces so as to show others that they are fasting. Truly I tell you, they have received their reward. But when you fast, put oil on your head and wash your face, so that your fasting may be seen not by others . . ." (Matthew 6:16-18a).

Worship

In corporate worship we hear the Scripture read and preached. We participate in baptism and Holy Communion. We sing our beliefs in the great hymns of the church, and we bring our offering and prayers to God. All this takes place in a setting rich in the visual symbols of our faith. In the sanctuary as we worship are the cross and the Bible and lighted candles representing the light of Christ. Some sanctuaries are themselves built in the shape of the cross. Present on the altar are the cup and bread. In banners or windows or carved into woodwork we may see the symbols of a fish, crown, or lamb, ancient symbols for Christ. These elements combine to bring us into a deeper perception of the God we worship.

Baptism and Holy Communion, as we noted at the beginning of this chapter, are great mysteries in which we come close to God. They are at the very center of Christian worship. These two sacred moments are essential to my life of faith, but I will never fully understand them. When I was a young child, a wise person told me that the sacraments—Holy Communion and baptism—are windows through which we glimpse God. As an adult, I have learned that the sacraments are signs and symbols of God's gracious action in our lives.

In Communion we gather at the table to be fed as a community and to come closer to God as individuals. Reflecting on our experience of the sacraments, and the other elements of worship, increases our understanding of our relationship to God. Such reflection can also enrich the worship experience. We might ask ourselves, "How was I called to greater discipleship by what occurred in worship this week? How do I respond to the gift of the Lord's Supper? How did the Scripture or music speak to me of God and my relationship to God?" Talking about these issues in conversation with friends or recording your response to worship in a journal is a habit worth cultivating. We will talk more about this sort of conversation later in this chapter.

Service to Others

We serve others in many ways. When Wesley talked about service as a means of grace, he was speaking particularly about service to those on the margins of our communities. Whether it is in a food pantry or a homeless shelter or an afterschool program for at-risk youth, we grow in faith when we attend to the needs of others. One of the most satisfying and popular ways of being in mission is the construction team. Teams from churches and businesses build homes, renew buildings, perhaps add handicapped ramps in many places.

A mission team from Bulverde United Methodist Church has spent time the last four summers on construction teams in the Rio Grande Valley of Texas and Mexico. This past summer a forty-member youth and adult team helped a family in LaJoya to build a one-thousand-square-foot home. They began praying for their mission, and the family they would serve, early in the year. The new house they built has an indoor bathroom and the first indoor running water this family has had in a home. In the rooms of their clean new home, this family cooks, eats, lives, and sleeps. As one member of the team said, "God called us down here to help these people have a home." That is what they did. They came back blessed by the joy and love of the family with whom they worked, and by the knowledge that God had used them.

It has taken time for the Bulverde team to reach this point in their mission experience. Four years ago, their first team of twenty people went to the project with few construction skills and little real knowledge of what they would find. They were there because their leader thought it would be "a good thing to do." The group was overwhelmed by the poverty they saw and by their opportunity to help. They determined to return and work the next year. Through their work and worship and fellowship the team learned a valuable lesson: the gift of grace is multiplied as it is shared. Their lives were changed as they discovered that God is at work in the world in ways we do not expect and often do not understand.

As they have learned over three summers to work as a team in construction, the group has also grown together in faith. Through their mission experience they have come to a place where they sense God's calling to them as a group and as individuals. They are aware of God's presence with them in what they do. The original team of twenty has grown to forty, with more waiting to participate. Hands-on service has become an important part of their Christian lives. Next summer they will take at least two teams to work in another part of the country, following God's calling.

Why can construction teams be so successful as places of Christian formation? A primary element is the group's devotional life. The team members from Bulverde have learned to make prayer and reflection part of their work pattern. They have shared their deepest needs and concerns as they prayed with a Christ candle each night. They have listened for God. Their leader, Cynthia Deaton, speaks of another important element in their success. "There are not many places in life today where we can see the results of our work. On a mission like this one, participants have an opportunity to see one project through to completion. They see concrete results of what they have done. They know that because of them, a family can live in clean, comfortable surroundings."

The members of the mission team from Bulverde, participating in the means of grace, have blessed the lives of the families for whom they have worked. They have also blessed the life of their congregation by their growing faith and their example.

Christian Conferencing

Christian conferencing is simply gathering with like-minded people for the purpose of reflecting on our life of faith. Wesley believed that faith grows in the midst of community. That community is experienced in corporate worship. Equally important is the small community of believers where Christian conferencing, talking about our life of faith intentionally, takes place. The mission team from Bulverde reflected together on their experience of ministry. That was an essential part of their growth experience. Like prayer and searching the Scripture, reflecting together is a means of grace because it can help us to greater consciousness of God's gracious activity. We pray or search the Scriptures or fast alone or as part of a group. As a community, we worship, participate in the sacraments, and perform service to others. These practices are means of grace for the community and for individuals. In Christian conferencing, we can reflect on God's action in our lives and on our response to God.

In Christian conferencing, we ask the "How is your soul?" questions. We listen to one another's experiences of God's grace and hold one another accountable in our listening for God and heeding God's word to us. This conversation may take place in a Covenant Discipleship Group or in a group formed for the purpose of spiritual formation. Christian conferencing may take place in a weekly Sunday school class or a support group for young mothers. Any setting where faith and the life of faith is the primary topic of conversation can be a setting for Christian conferencing. Christian conferencing may also be a conversation between two or three who are spiritual friends and who meet on a consistent basis to share their faith and support one another. Or, it could be a conversation between an individual and a spiritual director. Christian conferencing is a means of grace because it supports and reinforces our growing relationship with God and awareness of God's grace in our lives.

Means of Grace in Congregational Life

Christian formation is the process through which we are shaped into the likeness of Christ. Means of grace are those practices that strengthen and enrich our relationship to God in Christ and open us to being formed and shaped by God.

The congregation whose members live in close relationship to God, following God's leading in all they do, can have a powerful effect in the communities where they live and minister. In the remainder of this book, we will explore ways in which the means of grace can be practiced throughout the small-group life of the congregation. We will examine strategies to introduce Christian formation into the life of every committee and work group so that the church's primary mission of making disciples for Jesus Christ is carried out more effectively.

The stories and ideas in this book can help you in your service as a leader in your congregation's life. Use it to encourage and inform your own practice of holy habits. Use it as you plan strategies to help make your class, committee, or other small group a place where disciples are shaped and empowered for ministry.

We experience God's gracious love in many ways. There are some particular ways (means) through which Christians can become open to God's grace in their lives. Some of these means of grace are:
- corporate and personal worship.
- searching and studying the Scriptures.
- conversation with other Christians about where we see God working in our lives and what God is calling us to do (Christian conferencing).
- fasting.
- service to others, particularly the least among us.
- prayer.
- participation in the sacraments of baptism and Holy Communion.

Which means of grace are you currently practicing? Which means of grace are practiced in the small groups you are a part of? How does the experience of God's grace affect the life of your small groups?

Chapter Three

Accountability Groups

But speaking the truth in love, we must grow up in every way into him who is the head, into Christ.

Ephesians 4:15

I collect rocks, and return from every road trip loaded down with small stones to polish and give to friends. My favorite is the Petoskey stone, from the northern area of the lower Michigan peninsula. Three hundred fifty million years ago this area was a warm inland sea inhabited by a variety of tube-dwelling colony coral. These tiny creatures lived on micro-food pulled from the rich soup of sea water with their waving tentacles. As the earth changed and this sea dried up, the creatures died, leaving behind countless skeletons of their tube colonies. Today the skeletons are found in the rocks people call Petoskey stones. Polished with care, they are beautiful reminders of our planet's past, and lovely in their own right. Each one is unique.

Like Petoskey stones every human being is unique and beautiful. We are each also a reminder of our Creator. Each of us is shaped by life—and sometimes it almost feels as if we are being tumbled like stones in a polisher! But unlike rocks, we human beings do not have to be the totally passive subjects of life's working on us. We can work with God as each of us is formed into the uniquely beautiful creation God intends for us to be.

Accountability and Grace

Christian conferencing is a fundamental part of accountability groups. Accountability groups are meant to open participants to experience God's grace by making them accountable for learning and practicing holy habits. In accountability groups the sole focus is Christian formation. In these settings, people meet to support and encourage one another in the journey of faith. They encourage one another to keep patterns of prayer. They search the Scriptures together. They share stories of God's grace in their lives. Accountability groups are settings where we can hold one another accountable for the ways we live out our faith in the world and for practicing the means of grace.

Accountability groups come in many shapes and sizes, from small informal covenant groups like the one I belonged to (see page 6) to the more formal Covenant Discipleship Groups. Several types of accountability groups are described on the following pages. Sometimes the group forms intentionally, with people who share many elements of life in common. Sometimes they come together rather randomly, with membership based upon times available for meeting. All of these groups share one common quality: relationship to God is at the center.

Covenant Discipleship Groups

John Wesley knew that powerful preaching alone would not form people as Christian disciples. He was convinced that growing Christians must be nurtured in some small, regular setting. The class meeting is one of the original accountability groups in the Wesleyan tradition. In the early Methodist societies, members were organized into small groups called classes. In a structured setting, members encouraged one another in their Christian life and held one another accountable for their practice of the means of grace. Each class was led by a more experienced Christian, called the class leader. The class leaders themselves met monthly for support and nurture—and accountability.

The agenda for each class meeting was unfailingly the same. They began with a prayer and a hymn. Members took note of persons who were absent. If the absence was unaccounted for, one person was assigned to discover what had kept each absent member from the meeting. That person was also to organize whatever assistance the class might need to provide. When this business was done, each class member had an opportunity to speak about the "state of his soul" that week. Perhaps there were problems in life or faith. Perhaps the person had good news to share. Whatever was important in that person's life became the focus of the group. When all had had an opportunity to speak, and to support one another, the meeting closed with prayer.

Covenant Discipleship Groups are a contemporary adaptation of the class meeting. Small groups meet weekly to hold one another accountable to a covenant that they have agreed upon. The covenant is based on the General Rule of Discipleship, "To witness to Jesus Christ in the world, and to follow his teachings through acts of compassion, justice, worship, and devotion, under the guidance of the Holy Spirit" (see *Guide for Covenant Discipleship Groups* by Gayle Turner Watson; Discipleship Resources, 2000; page 12).

Gayle Turner Watson's *Guide for Covenant Discipleship Groups* provides an excellent guide for churches that are interested in establishing Covenant Discipleship Groups. For questions or additional information on Covenant Discipleship Groups, see the General Board of Discipleship's website (www.gbod.org) or contact the Office of Accountable Discipleship, General Board of Discipleship, P.O. Box 340003, Nashville, TN 37203-0003.

Emmaus Reunion Group

The Emmaus reunion group is another modern example of the class meeting format. Designed for people who have attended Walk to Emmaus (a weekend spiritual renewal program), the reunion group is made up of six to ten people who meet together weekly. It is highly structured, with a standard opening prayer and an agenda that provides each member an opportunity to speak on designated facets of his or her life. Participation in a reunion group has been a powerful formational experience in my own life. The members of the Viva Monday Morning Reunion—Dinah, Aleene, Molly, Martha, Liz, and I—have prayed our way through job changes, victories and defeats, death and living. We have made God's grace known to one another through a dozen years. We have held one another accountable for our lives of faith and loved and forgiven one another in so many varied circumstances.

Another Emmaus reunion group I know of in San Antonio began about ten years ago. It meets at 7:00 AM each Thursday morning at a popular restaurant, and members have breakfast together before their work day begins. There have been changes over the years as members have died or moved away and new people have come. Generally eight men and women meet around this breakfast table to share their faith and their lives in Christ. Thad says the group has a high priority in his life. "I arrange my travel and business schedule so that I can always be here, no matter what," he says.

Why is the group so important to its members? "This is like my family," says Bill. "The reunion group is a place where I am safe to share my Christian life" is Tom's feeling. Sue says, "Knowing I will meet in the Reunion each week requires me to reflect on my life—how I live my faith each day. The stories I hear from my friends each week inspire my own Christian life."

In the group, each person is listened to carefully, and there is always some helpful response. Each member is expected to share the moment during the week when he or she felt closest to Christ; a time when he or she represented Christ to another person by word or action; a time when an opportunity for discipleship was denied. Mike says of his reunion experience, "It feeds my soul." In addition to talking together, the group covenants to pray for one another each day and to pray for shared concerns. They carry out service to others as a group.

This group is in prayer for the community around them. Their prayer is often translated into action. Recently they prayed for a woman whose mother's death had left her with a run-down house to sell and no funds for repairs. The next week they gave their Saturday to tear down a ruined shed and build a back fence on the property so it could be sold. They are all involved with some kind of mentoring of older children and teenagers. Participants with whom I had conversation all agree that their reunion group gives them a sense of support and a place to be held to account as they live as Christian disciples.

For questions or additional information on Walk to Emmaus, access the Emmaus web site (www.upperroom.org/emmaus).

Other Accountability Settings

There are accountability groups other than Emmaus reunion groups or Covenant Discipleship Groups. The one of which I was a part, and wrote about in the first chapter, followed a simple covenant that one of the members wrote when we started. In our meetings each week we listened to one another's experience of faith during the week and talked about our lives of prayer. We prayed for one another and the world. We encouraged and challenged one another. Finally, we searched the Scriptures together, letting our lives encounter the Word for each of our situations.

There are many formats—and many terms—for accountability groups. You will hear them called small-group ministry in some areas, spiritual formation groups in others. The shared characteristic of all these experiences is that members hold one another accountable to the group and to God. In addition they all in one way or another encourage persons in growing spiritually.

If you want to encourage the beginning of accountability groups in your congregation there are many good resources available to help you and many ways to begin. In one church, the spiritual life committee sponsored short-term covenant groups as a Lenten activity. During that season, groups met once each week for prayer and reflection around the Scripture readings from the lectionary for Lent. Part of their covenant was daily prayer and devotional study of the lectionary readings at home. On Thursday of Holy Week, the groups participated in a thirty-six-hour time of prayer and fasting, which was broken with a Communion celebration followed by a common meal. Participants evaluated the experience at the end of the series. Most agreed that the covenant setting deepened their experience of Lent and their general openness to God.

Jo's Story

Several years ago, the spiritual life committee in one congregation decided to offer their members the opportunity to take part in formation/accountability groups. They began by holding a two-day weekend event. A leading writer in the field of spiritual formation in small groups was the featured speaker. In addition, there were workshops on prayer and journaling and several worship opportunities. At the end of the time, participants signed up for groups by putting the best day and time for them on a list. The staff then assigned persons to groups by choice of time and day.

Jo became part of a group with three other women whom she knew slightly. They were excited about the prospect of spiritual formation together and prepared for their first Wednesday evening meeting. The women decided to begin by using a popular spiritual formation workbook which included a set format they would follow each week. It included clear expectations for the group. The covenant that they developed included prayer for one another and for the community and time in study at home.

When they had completed the first workbook, the group felt they were finished with their "learning period" and ready to live in the accountability setting. They decided to continue without a set agenda or a covenant. They began a second study, one recommended by their staff person. Within a very few weeks, the character of the group changed. One or another of these busy women failed to do the home study one week. Another missed their meeting because of work or children's needs. One of the women entered into a time of crisis in her life, and the rest spent most of their meetings supporting her and offering advice and other assistance.

With no set expectations and no agenda, the group focus was lost. Members failed to make the meetings or study a priority in their busy lives. Whoever attended each week spent time in talking about the events in their lives and ways to support the ones who could not be there. Gone was any accountability, any searching the Scripture, any expectation of regular prayer or study. By the end of the first year the group had become close friends but agreed the formation group had not worked out. They decided to stop meeting on a regular basis. All were disappointed in the covenant experience, though they had gained valued friends.

Stumbling Blocks

The failure of Jo's covenant group experience illustrates the most common pitfalls that can undermine an accountability group. Knowing them before you begin can help your group stay "on course." These women had begun with a desire to know God more deeply, a clear agenda, and clear expectations. Jo and her friends had held one another accountable for lives of faith as they prayed for one another and the world. What had gone wrong? First, they failed to establish a permanent covenant. The basis of any kind of accountability group is the covenant to which all agree and which binds the group to God at its center. The covenant gives the group its continuing, recognized purpose. It is an anchor, a standard for the group.

In addition, Jo's group decided to work without an agenda. Experience has shown that desired outcomes seldom occur when there is no clear agenda, when meetings "just happen." Computer systems people have a saying, "If you don't know where you are going, you will probably wind up someplace else." That is true of any sort of accountability group.

As Jo's covenant group lost focus, members no longer made it a priority. The experience failed because it was no longer what the women had intended—or needed. Should you decide to undertake any kind of accountability group, you need not fail. Just remember to have clear expectations, stated and agreed to in a covenant promise, and a continuing, clear format for your meeting time to help you meet those expectations. There will be times when that format is swept aside in the face of some emergency. But over the long haul, keeping to an agenda is essential if a group is to fulfill its purpose.

Members also must be accountable to one another for keeping faithful to the habits that are part of their covenant, but there are dangers here as well. Sometimes folks can go overboard in the accountability department. They become intent on keeping one another accountable to the exclusion of everything else. It is essential to remember that the other side of the "accountability coin" is grace. That means sharing one another's stories of grace in our lives and celebrating. It means experiencing the grace and mercy of God together and sometimes through one another. It also means helping one another to be aware of and to access God's grace in all parts of our lives. When that balance is maintained, accountability groups become powerful elements in the spiritual formation of individuals.

Group Life Spans

It is helpful to remember that every group has a beginning and an end, and a life span in between. Because a group comes to an end eventually does not necessarily mean that it is not fruitful. Jo's formation group did not last because they did not maintain their focus, yet in many ways it was productive. All four women learned from their experience. They also formed lasting, valuable relationships with one another.

Sometimes a group dissolves because it has come to a logical ending place. The covenant group I was part of is an example. We broke up after about ten years, when two members moved away and others had greatly changed life and work circumstances. Because God was at the center, our experience of covenant relationship was pivotal in shaping us as Christian human beings. The relationships we formed in that group will be part of all our lives, part of who we are, for more years than we were together.

The experience of accountability groups can be life changing and faith forming for people in your congregation. If you do not have such experiences available, now is a good time to start!

John Wesley employed accountability groups as settings for Christian formation in the early Methodist Societies. Many accountability groups today include

- Christian conferencing, in which each person has an opportunity to speak about his or her experience of faith in that week, especially the ways in which faith deepened or the ways in which discipleship was denied, and hear comments from group members.
- a covenant to pray for one another and the greater community.
- service to others in Christ's name on a regular basis.
- caring for one another in times of illness or trouble.

Effective accountability groups

- have clearly stated objectives, often in the form of a written covenant.
- have a clear agenda and keep to it.
- are constant in prayer.
- make faithful attendance a priority.

Chapter Four

Learning Groups

Take my yoke upon you, and learn from me; for I am gentle and humble in heart, and you will find rest for your souls.

Matthew 11:29

From the two-year-olds in nursery school classes to senior adults in book discussion groups, learning is taking place in widely varied settings in congregations everywhere. Every learning setting can be a place of Christian formation—even for adults! We modern Americans have long had the notion that education is for information only. During the twentieth century, educators began to learn that there is more to learning than information. In the church that *more* is Christian formation—making the life of faith not something we learn about but something we learn to live.

The first hour of Wednesday Youth Club is always a noisy affair with lots of active games and horseplay. Children are burning off excess energy accumulated during a day of sitting still in school. In the second hour the children settle down, more or less, to Bible study. In Ruth's class, children sat very still on the Wednesday after Easter. "Now, take a deep breath and relax a little," Ruth said in a soft voice. Twelve tired bodies sagged. "Close your eyes, my dears, we are going on a trip in our imaginations." Twelve pairs of eyes closed, faces smiled. The children knew Ruth's imaginary journeys and liked them.

Speaking slowly and gently, Ruth began. "We are going to a garden this morning, a lovely spring garden. It is very cool in the garden this morning. I almost feel rain, or is it a mist? Smell the flowers and see the grass here! An early morning garden is such a lovely place. I wonder who takes care of this garden. Let's walk through the garden and listen for the sounds around us. There is something special in the air this morning. What do you feel in the air?" She paused.

"Is it excitement? Is it fear? Is it wondering?" Ruth paused for a longer moment. "There is a tomb on the other side of the garden. I wonder if you can see it from here? A tomb is a small sort of room dug out of the side of a hill, where people in Jesus' time placed those who had died. Can you see the stone rolled in front of the opening as a door?"

"I think I see someone coming. O my, it is a group of women and men, and the men are running! I wonder who they are. I wonder why they are running. Let's follow behind them in the garden and see what happens." She paused again. "They are running to the tomb! Oh, look—the tomb is open! The stone door is rolled away! I'm going to stand here a minute and watch to see what happens next. I wonder what will you do?" Ruth stopped talking and let the children sit in silence for a moment or so.

Now Ruth began to talk in her normal tone of voice. "Let's think about this garden for a minute, then we can talk together. I wonder what is happening here. I wonder what the people are feeling." Then she gave time for the children to think and begin to respond. When all of the children had had a chance to speak, Ruth suggested that they pray together. "How shall we pray?" she asked. The children made their suggestions, and the prayer began. In the prayer, Ruth might have said, "Thank you God for this morning when the tomb is open. Thank you for the people who cared about Jesus. Thank you that Jesus is risen for us! Thank you that I can love Jesus. Thank you for loving us. Amen."

Learning and Faith

The purpose of Christian education is to help people know and experience God through Jesus Christ, claim and live God's promises, and grow and serve as Christian disciples. That purpose was being fulfilled in the Youth Club fifth grade class on the Wednesday after Easter. The class heard the Resurrection story in a way that would help each one to remember it and begin to make it his or her own. Equally important, the children were learning how to pray together, how to be in conversation with God as a group. They were practicing prayer, Scripture study, and Christian conferencing in their learning environment. Christian formation was taking place.

Ruth creates her "Bible Journeys" out of her lifelong experience of Scripture and her personal relationship to God in Jesus Christ. Anyone, anywhere can have—or be—a teacher who makes use of study materials which focus on formation as well as information; one whose faith experience is the basis of his or her classroom teaching. Learning for formation shapes our spirits to be open to God in Christ. It involves different sorts of questions and activities than learning for information. Both kinds of learning are important for nurturing Christian discipleship.

As we seek to help people of every age learn to listen for God and to seek relationship with God, we need to provide experiences that help them listen for what God is saying to them. Hopefully we help them learn to hear the invitations God is making to us through the written Word. It is ultimately God who shapes us, but in this sort of teaching we are helping learners to adopt habits which will create openness to God's working in their lives. This is essential to their growing faith, their growing relationship to God.

For adults, one of the best models of formational learning is the DISCIPLE Bible study series. In each of the year-long DISCIPLE studies, students and teacher spend thirty-two weeks of disciplined study. Formational learning is combined with study for information. In each week's work, the student reads passages for content, learning the context and background of portions of Scripture. Then, he or she reads for the message to his or her own life situation. In this way, students learn a disciplined method of studying Scripture not only for learning but also for Scripture's encounter with their lives. In DISCIPLE, questions which lead to this encounter come under the heading of "Into the Word Into the World."

In addition, DISCIPLE study groups build a community in which members pray for one another's concerns each week, then discuss their prayer in each session. Their study at home begins each day with a prayer of praise and continues with intercession for others. A disciplined pattern of prayer is learned in this way over the thirty-two weeks of the study. Through the DISCIPLE group one can learn patterns of prayer, study, and reflection that are life changing.

Story and Faith

Christians are a people of stories. When we teach for information, we are helping learners in their task of knowing, understanding, and appropriating these stories. The Bible stories are the witness to God's work in the world in the people of Israel and in the life, death, and resurrection of Jesus Christ. The task of learning and understanding them is essential for growing faith.

When we teach formationally, our goal is to help people appropriate the Bible stories and make them part of their own lives—in other words, learn to listen for God's Word to each of them in the Bible stories. Formational teaching and learning may use a variety of teaching tools and methods. For example, opportunities for creative expression help learners to encounter the Bible stories at a formational level. There are many mediums for creative expression—from music and drama to paint on paper. One of my favorites is modeling compound. Modeling compound is a clean and easy to use variation on clay. It is available in white and several colors in many craft stores.

Several years ago I taught a new class for young couples, which we called Class Shalom. This lively group was full of lawyers and landscapers, work-at-home moms and businessmen, doctors and architects. The discussions in that group were often noisy and always interesting and challenging. But they seldom went deep, seldom reached a feeling level. The class stayed at an intellectual place, with the members challenging one another at every point. It was an enjoyable learning experience, but it was not formational.

Then one Sunday I brought some modeling compound to class. At every place as people arrived was a plastic bag filled with the white substance. I had labeled it as material for a creative project "later." By the time the business and opening prayer were over, every bag was opened! As the class members manipulated clay almost unconsciously, they entered into discussion at a new and deeper level. Soon, people were talking about their lives of faith, and the ways the Bible lesson had intersected their lives that week. At the end of the time, I asked the class to look at the clay they held, and talk in pairs about the creations they had formed.

The reports of those conversations were almost unanimous in one comment. No one in the class had really formed anything consciously. Instead, as they worked the clay, class members had found their minds were free to encounter the lesson material in new ways. Whatever had been made was created unconsciously as learners reflected and talked. The process had been more important than any end product. That day was a turning point for the class. It has become, over the years and with a succession of teachers, a powerful place of Christian formation. Many of the current leaders in our congregation come from Class Shalom. They are leaders who are taking us into stronger discipleship as a congregation.

Dan and Nancy and Class Shalom

Dan and Nancy have been part of Class Shalom for eight years. I talked with them about their experience of the class. Dan, who is currently the lead teacher, remarked that the class is sometimes formative intentionally, sometimes almost by accident. Nancy says the sense of Christian community seems to be the strongest element in her own formation in the class. She remembers people bringing food and "being there" when she had heart problems. Dan mentioned the dynamic of a diversity of strong opinions and there being room for all. "I find great openness to all shades of opinion in the class sessions," he said.

"There is great caring for one another in Class Shalom and also reinforcing one another's values—even when they disagree. This is a group where they all seem to place less importance on material possessions and exercise stewardship over their money," Nancy commented. "For example, many class members are affluent couples who drive used cars and tithe their incomes." They spend many hours in "hands-on" service and support ventures like sending a trio of disadvantaged Hispanic children to a Christ-centered camp each summer.

Earlier this year, Dan and Nancy started visiting other churches. They were looking for a congregation with a larger youth program for their two children. They have decided to remain at their current church largely because of Class Shalom. They could not find anywhere else a Sunday school class with the same sense of community, diversity, and support of Christian values that they know in their class.

The Habit of Prayer in Learning Settings

One of the formative elements in Class Shalom from the beginning has been prayer—prayer in the class and prayer when they are separated. They pray for one another and for the church, for the community and for the world. Prayer has helped to shape their character. Just as prayer shapes individuals, praying together shapes any group. Over time, the group that prays together—for one another, and for the community outside the group—creates bonds of caring for one another that are not easily broken. One individual's concerns become shared concerns. One person's celebrations become group celebrations. Out of this concern and caring for one another can grow the habit of concern for the community outside the group. Concern for community beyond themselves can precipitate active "hands-on" ministry to others. God-centered relationship within a learning setting can lead to involvement in the hurt and need of a broken world.

How can leaders develop the habit of prayer in learning settings? First you might want to come to agreement within the group that you will begin and end your sessions with prayer consistently. This is possible even with young children. Try different patterns of prayer for a few weeks to see what is most fitting for your group. The first week, you might try starting the class with a circle of concern, each person voicing his or her prayer concern and the group responding with "Lord, hear our prayer" or another sentence. With younger learners, you might begin with a circle of sentence prayers of thanksgiving. In this way, you will begin your session acknowledging and welcoming God's presence. You will also probably clear people's minds to concentrate on the lesson! At the close of your time, you might invite each participant to pray a sentence prayer growing out of their understanding of the lesson. Simply call the group to an attitude of prayer, invite sentence prayers growing out of the lesson, and then wait in silence for the first prayer. If this is not comfortable, you might invite the class members to go round the table or circle in order (always allowing for the option of passing without praying aloud). One person can be selected to close the prayer time with a simple benediction or dismissal.

Another time, you might ask one student to open the session by reading a Psalm, perhaps Psalm 121 or 131, and then have a moment or two of silence so that people may pray silently in response to the reading. Invite learners into a circle for prayers of concern at the end of your class time. You may choose to end this circle with the same sung or spoken blessing each week.

Sometimes the teaching materials your class is using will have opening and closing prayer planned as part of the session. Use those if you are at ease with them, but don't let teaching materials dictate to you how your class will pray. As you consider the material you are teaching and your class makeup, ideas for ways to pray will rise in your mind. Pay attention to them! The class members themselves often will be your best resource as you consider how to make prayer a habit in your particular learning setting.

Experiential Learning and Formation

Learning for formation does not always happen in a classroom. Church holidays—holy days—present special opportunities for formational learning.

One year while I was on staff at a large downtown church, Christmas fell on a Sunday. The question at one staff meeting was what to do for Sunday school. We knew attendance would probably be low on that day. Someone suggested we cancel Sunday school and try an intergenerational "create as we go" Christmas pageant during the worship hour. Our brave pastor said OK, and the planning began.

As the education committee and children's council met together we decided to hold a happy birthday party at the Sunday school hour. We would have decorations, a cake with candles, and punch and coffee. As people arrived, they would choose a token which would denote their role in the worship-hour pageant. Some people would be shepherds, some animals, some trees or stars, some angels. The choir would be "planted" in the angel group, and the parents of a new baby in the church would be Mary and Joseph with their child as the baby Jesus.

After the Christmas Eve service, some people stayed to remove the pulpit, choir chairs, and altar. In their places on the now bare platform they arranged bales of hay and a manger. Behind all these the large wooden cross hung in its place high on the front wall. On Sunday morning the staff and planning committee gathered, our work complete. As people began to arrive for Sunday school—more than we had expected—youth handed them tokens and information sheets, and in some cases costumes. We ate cake and drank coffee and punch, and played games like "Pin the Baby in the Manger." We sang Christmas carols accompanied by a guitar-playing youth.

Shortly before 11:00 AM we were ready to introduce the Christmas Pageant. After some explanation, everyone walked together into the sanctuary. There was the altar area, bare of its usual furnishings and dominated by the Christmas tree at one side of the front, the manger and hay bales at the other, and the great wooden cross hanging over it all. Pastor Dan, in street clothes, said good morning and led us in a prayer of thanksgiving. Then he began to read the beautiful words of the story of Jesus' birth from the Gospel of Luke. Mary and Joseph and the baby came in and took their places—the baby cooing and waving his small hands! As Dan read, the stars took their places behind the family, and trees and animals came to join in as well.

"In that region there were shepherds living in the fields," Dan read, and shepherds moved to stand at one side of the front. As Dan read on, "Then an angel of the Lord appeared before them," the choir and other angels from the congregation walked up to the front and began to sing, "Gloria in Excelsis Deo." "Let us go now to Bethlehem and see this thing that has taken place," read Dan. "So they went with haste."

Then all the shepherds in their bathrobe costumes came to kneel at the communion rail. I knelt next to an eighty-year-old woman from the women's Bible study class. I had known her to be faithful in attendance and in outreach to others for many years. She seemed to be a model of discipleship, except that she was a particularly joyless person. As I watched on this Christmas morning, she knelt with tears running down her cheeks. Then she turned to me, smiling through her tears. "I never realized until today what all this Christmas stuff really means," she said. "He came for me!"

I don't know for certain what anyone else learned on that Sunday, though I heard all sorts of stories from others who were there. I do know about my friend from the Bible study class. I will never forget her face that morning, and the powerful learning she did on that Christmas day. My elderly friend found new life in an impromptu Christmas morning pageant. She learned that God had sent Jesus for her salvation, and her life after that was filled with joy.

One does not need to be in a large church with a professional staff to teach experientially. It doesn't have to happen at Christmastime in the sanctuary. We all have the opportunity to help people of any age open their hearts to learn from Jesus and be formed in his image. Any time teachers and leaders follow the Spirit's leading to plan experiential learning around the holy days of the Christian year this kind of learning can happen.

If you are not comfortable with experiential learning, chances are you can find at least one person in your congregation who is. Use stories with classes of every age! Invite a good storyteller into your adult class to tell the story of blind Bartimaeus, then tell it again as learners create pantomimes.

Encourage a group of fifth graders to act out the Pentecost drama or set the kindergarten class free with the same narrative. Use a "story box" with wood or paper characters or a puppet stage and puppets set up in a doorway. Children, youth, or adults can re-enact the stories they have heard and experience them in new ways.

Teachers and Formation

Christian formation in a learning setting doesn't always need particular materials. Sometimes the teacher himself or herself is the "curriculum." My favorite Sunday school teacher is Aleene Block. Aleene has been praying, searching the Scriptures, and living in service to others for the whole of her long life. Her faith—her relationship to God—is deep and strong. She has been teaching an adult class for many years. Aleene shares her faith with the class. She challenges us to search and listen for what God is saying to us in each week's lesson, whatever written material we use.

The class closes with a circle of prayer and a sung blessing each time they meet. They pray for one another during the week. They engage in ministry to those outside their own circle on a regular basis. With Aleene's leading, they have made these means of grace a part of our class life.

Incorporating the Means of Grace

You can make the means of grace a regular part of your youth or adult learning group whether it be Sunday school or another learning group. How this happens will depend on your teaching style, but there are a few "rules of thumb" you might want to follow as you begin. First, make it a habit, if you are not already doing so, to begin and end every class session with prayer.

Next, develop and encourage in your class the habit of ministry to others—whatever the age group. Plan two or more mission/service activities during each year. You may choose to be in ministry together to someone within the church family or to people in the greater community. Begin your work time with prayer, asking God to be present as you work and to bless those whom you serve.

Let your ministry together lead to Christian conferencing, another means of grace. In the class session following your mission activity, talk about it in class. You might want to ask questions like "How was God present in our work together?" or "How was God's love made evident to those whom we served?" or "How might we continue in ministry to them in Christ's name?" or "How does sharing the love of Christ in your community increase your own awareness of God's presence in your midst?" This Christian conference around your mission experience will be valuable to your class in ways that will reach beyond the activity itself.

A third thing you want to consider is attending worship as a group on one Sunday each quarter. Participating in worship together and talking about it afterwards can make the service of worship even more meaningful. You might want to center an "after-worship" conversation around the symbols visible in the Sanctuary or the hymns and anthems sung that day. How did those elements add to your perception of God's Word to you in the worship, or increase your appreciation of the Scripture and preaching?

Finally, let the lessons you teach lead to searching the Scriptures for God's word to each member that day. The way you lead into discussion can enable students to listen for God's invitation to them that day.

Developing a Teacher's Best Resource

The finest resource you have in teaching or leading any class is your own life of faith. The best way to begin making your class a place of formation is to look at your own practice of "holy habits" and make them a part of your daily life. You will find your relationship to Christ growing and deepening as this preparation continues.

An excellent tool to help you in this process is Carol Krau's book *Keeping in Touch*, which is listed in the Resource section. Perhaps you may want to get together with other teachers to study this book together as one way to deepen your faith. You may decide to invite your pastor or some other church leader to meet with you.

Your own practice of the means of grace will be the best preparation for you teachers who want to make your classes places where people learn to be open to the shaping power of the Holy Spirit. As you learn to take the yoke of Jesus upon you and learn from him, learners in your class will follow your example. Teaching—and learning—will be filled with new meaning and a new joy.

Learning settings are most often seen as informational in the secular world. In the congregation, Christian formation is an essential element in the learning setting. In order for learning to be formational, learners must be encouraged to go beyond information to deeper meanings and to feelings.

At every age level, they can be helped to make this transition through the use of:

- creative activities like using clay or drawing to express their feelings about the meaning of a Bible story.
- drama, music, and dance that draw people into the faith story.
- open-ended discussion that helps people to draw out their deeper feelings instead of looking for "right answers."
- simple guided meditations based on a Bible story.
- opportunities for worship and prayer in the classroom.

There are countless resources for making a learning setting more formational. The most important one is the teacher's own developing faith.

Asking yourself these questions will help you put the ideas in this chapter to work in your own setting:

- How can I add creative activities to the setting where I teach in ways that will open learners to God's forming activity?
- Who are people in the congregation who can help me?
- Where can I find the resources I might need?
- How can I begin to take the development of my own faith more seriously?

Chapter Five

Serving Groups

And whatever you do, in word or deed, do everything in the name of the Lord Jesus, giving thanks to God the Father through him.

Colossians 3:17

Perhaps the largest set of small groups in your congregation is made up of people who serve others in one way or another. They may be some variation of a kitchen guild or a mission work team. They may be choir singers or bell ringers or people who visit the sick. They may keep track of your emergency community food pantry or sew banners for the sanctuary. They may drive vans or pull weeds or change light bulbs. Whatever they do, these groups carry out much of the "hands-on" work of the church.

As we serve others out of our love of Christ, we can become more aware of God's grace in our own lives and the lives of those we serve. For instance, Barbara leads a group of volunteer teachers in presenting a Bible school at a mission outpost in Central America each summer. As part of this ministry, she has learned to lean on God in her own need. She has seen God at work in the unchurched children who come to Bible school. She has observed God's mercy and grace in the lives of the missionaries in Guyana. She has experienced God's love in the children.

Barb says of the first year's adventure, "We left San Antonio thinking we were taking God to poor underprivileged children in Guyana. We got there and found God waiting for us in the children! And before we left we had seen and felt God's presence in all our lives. The experience will always be more, much more, than we could ever have expected."

In South Texas, where flash flooding is commonplace, many rural buildings are erected on piling foundations. Ted spent the better part of one year as the leader of a team working to rebuild a tiny church ripped apart by a terrible storm in the fall of 1998. Early in 1999, a newspaper in San Antonio ran the story of New Jerusalem Church, located in a rural area just outside the city. The structure had been blown nearly off its foundation during the storm. It was resting precariously on the pilings, the floor was slanted, and the roof had been damaged by winds. Most of the windows were broken, and there had been damage to interior walls as well. The front porch was about gone. The small congregation feared they would have to leave their church home permanently.

Over a period of ten months, a team composed of people from several congregations worked many Saturdays to repair and rehabilitate this small community church. Rebuilding this worship space, members of the team have built new relationships within their own family of faith.

For all of us who worked, that year changed lives. Worshiping in the building on the congregation's first day back, we all agreed that we experienced the presence of God in new and deeper ways. It was more than satisfaction at seeing our work complete. It was much more than knowing that the sturdy building, shiny new windows, and comfortable pews were our handiwork. We had shared in building a small part of the Kingdom on earth.

At lunch with other members of the team after worship, we had an opportunity to reflect together on the work we had done. As we ate barbecue and potato salad, the group talked about the ways God had used us and our various gifts to repair this place of worship. We talked about the people who had come to worship, about the child in a wheelchair who had used the ramp that had been built.

In leading this small group of construction volunteers, Ted was formed and shaped by God as he worked to reconstruct a small country church. Barb was formed more closely into the image of God as she worked with the small group of VBS teachers and the resident missionary in Guyana. Christian service is itself a means of grace, bringing us closer to God and to one another.

Groups Who Serve Others

Tom has been part of the Lunch Bunch crew for fifteen years now, since he took early retirement at age sixty. The folks on this crew cook, serve, and clean up from lunch for 150-200 senior citizens every Thursday at a local church. They are all—table servers, cooks, and dishwashers—volunteers who miss working each week only if they are away or ill, although the oldest is in her eighties. Thursday is a day they look forward to. Their participation has helped to shape their lives in the twenty years the Lunch Bunch has been going on. The workers have become a small Christian community, concerned for one another outside of their work setting.

The Lunch Bunch crew experience has had a profound impact on participants like Wanda. She says, "I love working in the Lunch Bunch crew! We can see the results of our work in the faces of the people who come for lunch week after week. They come early to meet friends they have made here, and talk. They get a good meal for a reasonable cost. This is an important work we do!"

More Than Labor

Many serving groups have been working together for a long while, like the Lunch Bunch crew. Others may come together for a Habitat for Humanity home or some other short-term effort. There is often much more than labor involved when groups gather to serve. Whether short-term or continuing, groups whose primary purpose is service can be powerful instruments for spiritual formation.

The experience of youth mission teams in South Texas is one example of the way formation happens in groups who serve others. Our youth group members are probably typical of the teenagers who form youth mission teams. They are a sometimes rowdy collection of young people from varying backgrounds and several schools. Some of them sing in choir, and most of them participate in a yearly drama/music production in some way. Many of them are in Sunday school at least part of the time. Most of them participate in the yearly mission service project trip to the Rio Grande Valley.

Texas and Mexico meet in the valley of the Rio Grande. There is great poverty among workers in the favelas "across the river." This year is the fourth summer our youth have gone down to the valley to build small homes for families there. Each year the youth have come home awed by and eager to talk about the mission trip. This undertaking has profoundly affected their understanding of themselves as Christians—and their understanding of God. The annual experience of mission is a highlight of their summer. It is the primary time of growth in their faith and in their sense of themselves as a community of Christians.

The mission team this year is composed of twenty youth led by five adults including the youth director, two people experienced in construction, a Spanish-speaker who is in charge of the Bible story hour they will conduct on Thursday afternoon, and the team leader. On a Sunday morning early in June, the mission team is dedicated in worship, then leaves for the Valley.

They will spend the week living in a Volunteers in Mission camp on the Texas side of the Rio Grande, about an hour's drive away from the work site in Rio Bravo, Mexico.

Each day they rise before dawn for breakfast and clean-up, pack a lunch and lots of water, and set out. On the way to the site, they collect the two Mexican "foremen" who will guide their work. By 8:30 on the first day they are at work at the concrete slab that will become a house. At noon they will stop for lunch, then continue until about 3:00 PM when intense heat drives everyone into the shade to rest. At the end of that first day cement-brick walls will have been started, and the house will begin to take shape. When it is complete the simple home will have two rooms, each with a glass window, and a secure front door.

For the family who will live in the finished house, it will be the first time they have space of their own. Family members will come to work with the mission team as they have free hours from their own jobs. Children of the family may come to watch in excitement, sometimes bringing a drink of lemonade or fruit juice for the workers. Future neighbors may offer a hand or stop to visit with volunteers. By Tuesday afternoon, the walls will be up and windows ready to install. Some people will begin to frame and lay the tin roof. By noon on Thursday, all that will be left to do is the clean-up—and installing the front door.

The youth and adults have worked prodigiously, creating a small home in three and a half days in searing heat. From youngest junior high student to the just graduated seniors, they have all worked together, teaching one another and sharing the load. Sometimes they have to stop for extra drinks of Gatorade or to tend to hammer-hit fingers or scraped knees. Sometimes a smaller seventh grader staggers under the weight of a concrete block, or grows dizzy trying to climb up to the roof. There is always another youth there to help. The group has become a working community where every contribution is valued.

On Thursday afternoon, the team will take a break and hold a short Bible school for neighborhood children. They have brought Bible story books in Spanish to give as gifts as well as activities centered around the stories they will tell. Those who are not fluent in Spanish practice phrases they will need until they are letter perfect.

Back at the camp each evening, after everyone has had a shower or a swim, and supper, there is time for recreation. This summer someone brought a chess board and pieces. A continuous, seriously fought tournament goes on throughout the week, and the board is seldom idle when the team is not at work.

Before they go to bed each night, the group gathers in quiet to reflect on their day in light of Scripture and to pray. Youth members of the team have prepared for each evening's time. Led by the youth, the group prays for those they serve, for the ones they left at home, and for one another. To close their time of reflection and prayer, the group passes a Christ candle. As each person takes the candle, he or she "has the floor." In this prayerful atmosphere youth and adults are free to say whatever is on their hearts. They all know that whatever they say will be in confidence and will be heard without comment. Occasionally one person will touch the hand of another, or the group will gather around one who is obviously hurting to offer comfort and prayer. When all have had a chance to speak, the group sings a benediction and they go off to bed—teasing and jostling on the way!

On Friday their week of service will be over. In the morning they will give the windows of the new home a final polish, sweep the floor and lay down reed matting, then present the keys and a new Bible to the proud family. They will have lunch with other mission teams, giving thanks in corporate worship for the gifts of the week. Then our group will head off for thirty-six hours at the beach.

Remembering what has happened because they allowed God to move through them has changed the lives of these young people. They have been shaped profoundly by the experience of mission. Reflecting each day, praying for one another and for those they served, letting their work be informed by encounter with Scripture, they have been further shaped in the image of God.

The story of the Laurel Heights Youth Mission Team contains all the elements that can make any serving group a powerful place of Christian formation. Those means of grace are work in Christ's name, corporate and individual prayer, searching the Scripture and reflection as a group, and celebration together.

One key to Christian formation in any group whose purpose is service is to be sure that everyone is clear on the reason for undertaking the work they do. The Thursday Lunch Bunch crew cooks to feed senior citizens, and they know the reason they cook that lunch is to offer their patrons the hospitality of Christ.

When vacation Bible school leaders and teachers plan and prepare intensely for weeks and then travel a thousand miles to teach in a mission school, it is not solely to entertain young children. They labor to bring children an experience of the love of God in Christ. The team rebuilding New Jerusalem Church was working to the glory of God in their construction. Leaders can help to reinforce this awareness among every member of every group that works to serve others in Christ's name. One way is to begin and end every work or planning or conversation session with prayer. One simple method might be to open the group's activity each time they meet with a prayer circle. Perhaps a different person might lead prayer each time the group meets to work. This opening prayer might include concerns of the members as well as celebrations and a prayer asking God to bless the work of the day.

A brief time of prayer at the end of the day might give thanks for the gift of labor in Christ's name, intercede for those for whom you have worked, and ask the blessing of rest for the work team. Again, a different person might lead each time. Leaders might also encourage their teams to pray for those they are serving during private prayer at home.

"Brief" is an important word in the work setting. To be effective, prayer does not have to go on for fifteen or twenty minutes. Five to ten minutes at the beginning of the day with everyone focused on prayer will do the job! The same is true of prayer time at the end of a work session. Five focused minutes is enough to give thanks and celebrate work together.

Reflection together is another tool for reinforcing awareness of the reasons for your work. It is not going to be easy to find time to reflect in the light of Scripture when all the members of a work team have busy lives. Where it is at all possible, make this reflection part of the work day. One example of this is the annual Habitat work weeks that Tom and his friends have attended. San Antonio Habitat for Humanity cooperates with local church and business groups for a two-week construction effort that results in ten to twenty-five new homes each year. Teams have built whole new neighborhoods near the center of the city with this effort. During the two-week period, teams began their work day with breakfast provided by volunteers. Along with the meal, there was opportunity for reflection on the daily task in light of the Word, presented by a different group leader each day. Some people came late and missed the meal and reflection, but opportunity was there every day. Several people who missed breakfast and reflection on the first day heard about it from others and came earlier. Many did not. For those who got up early for breakfast and reflected together, it was a rich and rewarding time.

Ongoing groups may take one meeting every few weeks to reflect on their work within the context of the Word. The Lunch Bunch kitchen crew, for instance, eats lunch each week when all their clients are served. They might spend their luncheon hour in reflection and prayer once a month. Using the meal time as reflection will add to the activity's value for all who work. Again, the word in the work setting is *brief* time. One strategy for reflection at breakfast or lunch table would be to place a sheet with a Scripture quotation and one or two reflection questions at each place. When the group has finished eating, ask them to spend a minute or so in silence with the reading and questions, then talk in groups of two or three around the table. The conversation need take only another five or six minutes, and can be brought to closure with sharing in the large group or appropriate comments from the leader for the day.

The purpose of reflection in the work setting is not to dot every *i* or cross every *t* in an exposition of Scripture. The purpose is to give participants fuel for their personal reflection. The ideas they begin to generate during reflection time "on the job" will stay with them, and God will work in persons as they go on to the other activities of the day.

It may be appropriate to end reflection time with prayer. If so, prayer may grow out of the Scripture read. However the closing prayer time comes, it will send people away knowing they have worked in the presence of the One who created and is creating us day by day.

The final ingredient in the serving group's formation process is opportunity for celebration. In a relatively short-term group, like the team who rebuilt the New Jerusalem Church, celebration can be a natural outgrowth of the mission project. On the first Sunday the congregation was back in its worship space, it was appropriate for them to ask those who had rebuilt the structure to be present. It was appropriate to ask representatives of that team to take part in the worship. The experience of being together in worship capped the team's effort to rebuild. That day in worship is a time none of the team will forget very soon.

We have seen how formation can take place in groups formed to serve. In the stories of the youth mission team and the team who rebuilt the New Jerusalem Church we hear our own stories. In every congregation there are people like Barb and the VBS mission team, or Tom and Wanda and the Lunch Bunch crew.

What is it that causes a service group to take the extra steps that lead to powerful experiences of formation for its members? Usually it is leadership. When lay leadership is inclined—and equipped—to encourage prayer and reflection, searching the Scriptures, and group celebration, positive Christian formation will more than likely take place. It is the task of the church to prepare leaders for formation in all the work groups of the congregation. There are many written resources, and every worker from youth to the older adult can take a turn at leading prayer. The team leader must be the one who assigns leadership, makes resources available, and sets the example by considering this time important. When churches select teams and leadership for service, a necessary gift equal to skills of cooking or construction is the gift of prayer and reflection.

When we encourage and equip work teams for attention to Scripture and prayer the results will far outreach our expectations. Workers serving with glad and generous hearts will give glory to God. God will work powerfully in the midst of all our ministry teams, bringing members ever closer to one another and to the Source of our lives.

Service to others in Christ's name is itself a means of grace. There are several keys to making service groups important places of Christian formation:
- Make sure that every member of a work team is aware of the reason for undertaking the work they do. Everyone needs to be aware that what they are doing is ministry in Christ's name.
- Reflecting together in the context of Scripture keeps working groups focused on their context as servants of Christ.
- Prayer, for one another and for those they serve, is essential in the communal life of those in a group formed for service.
- Celebration of what the group has accomplished is another important element.
- Finally, leadership prepared to set an example in all these areas of reflection, searching the Scriptures, prayer, and celebration is key to a formational experience.

Chapter Six

Administrative Groups

Now you are the body of Christ and individually members of it.

1 Corinthians 12:27

As members of congregations everywhere, we undertake the ministry of administration and governance. In some ways, we look and act like any governing body anywhere. But we are more. Even—or perhaps especially—when we work at governance in the church we are the body of Christ. For us, governance is ministry. Our administrative work enables the day-to-day ministry we carry out in the world in Christ's name.

At times, in the throes of administrative detail and procedure, we begin to forget who and whose we are. When that happens, we become like any other organization. We are prey to all sorts of dissension and difficulty. Consider the church council of a large downtown church. The council had gathered to discuss and vote on the annual budget. That budget was being presented after months of work by the congregation's planning task force. It was a visionary budget to support a courageous plan for ministry. A long process of prayer and study had led the task force to propose a profound change in the ministry of the congregation. The plan was to reach out in Christ's name to inner-city neighborhoods as well as to workers in the buildings which surrounded the church.

Planning task force members approached this session with enthusiasm. They had listened for God's guidance, praying together weekly. They had studied the church's finances carefully. They had been faithful to their mandate to take the congregation in new directions. Their ministry plan would entail many changes, but they were confidant that it would lead the church to new levels of growth and participation. Unfortunately, they had forgotten some important steps in their work.

The congregation had not made input into any of the conversations as the task force studied and planned. Information about the budget and its concomitant goals had not been widely shared throughout the membership. Task force members had made no interim reports to the church council. There had been no mention in worship of the new plan or its supporting budget. No one outside the task force had had conversation, reflection, and prayer around the new goals.

The budget and ministry plan meeting agenda was full. There was no time set aside for prayer or reflection together. As soon as the meeting was called to order the budget and action plan was distributed. Little or no background was given on the task force's work and study. As discussion began there were many questions and objections. This new and radically different ministry plan appeared to threaten many members' deep feelings about their congregation and their perceived needs.

The meeting became a loudly contentious session. An "us" and "them" atmosphere developed in the room. People expressed their opinions in negative, sometimes hurtful statements. The budget proposal and ministry plan were tabled when it became clear there could be no agreement that evening. Several persons left the session feeling deeply distressed and alienated.

The outcome of this meeting was a failed plan, and a need for healing. Council members were angry and hurt. The planning task force felt betrayed by the congregation. How did this situation arise? At the most basic level, council members forgot that the real focus here was not money or change but ministry in Christ's name. When the church council met to vote on this ministry plan and budget they had not met as the body of Christ. They were not asked to consider the issues involved in the context of prayer and Scripture reflection. With no prior reflection on issues and no faith context, the meeting lost focus and degenerated into bickering. As a result, the meeting left participants feeling tired and bruised and lacking trust in their fellow council members or the planning task force. They no longer felt able to participate in governance at a meaningful level.

Individuals are shaped in some way by every experience we encounter. In contentious and sometimes bitter church meetings, that shaping is negative. We seem to learn that some people are less acceptable than others. We are taught by experience that the ideas of some people are of considerably less value than those of others. We learn that it is permissible to deride some people and welcome others. Certainly we are not shaped in the image of Christ in that kind of experience.

We have said that every meeting in any congregation could be a place of positive Christian formation. If we are to survive as a faithful people, this formation must happen in governance settings. Why is it that often the opposite is what occurs?

One reason may be the way we think about governance and administration in the church. We often tend to separate what is "religious" from what is "business." We think of administration in the church in secular terms and see programs and worship as "the religious part." We fail to remember that all the business of the church is ministry carried out in response to God's grace for us. We forget that what we do in the ministry of governance is intended to be not necessarily in our own interest but in the interest of the gospel of Jesus Christ. As a consequence, church administrative meetings at every level can become trapped in a tangle of personal feelings, hidden agendas, and false priorities. Out of these failures arises the lack of Christian formation in administrative settings in our congregations.

Church governance can be efficient and effective and also contribute to formation in the image of Christ. For this to happen, we must cease thinking of church business in secular terms. We must teach ourselves to see the business of the church as God's business. This is a tall order. How can we change our ways of working so that all of our administrative meetings are settings in which Christian formation occurs, so that in all committees and task forces of the church we follow God's leading? There are many paths congregations might follow to reach this goal.

One way to begin the process of making administrative sessions places of Christian formation is to ask some questions about governance in your congregation. Is listening emphasized as a leadership skill? Are you more concerned with issues than personalities in meetings? Are all members well-informed about the business of the committees with which they work? Is all your committee work informed and illuminated by encountering Scripture and reflecting on your task in that context? Is there opportunity to search the Scriptures together in every session? Is every meeting begun and continued in prayer? Are there people somewhere praying for the meeting while it is in session? Are committee or council members given the opportunity to pray for one another, and the congregation, between meetings?

The first three questions in the paragraph above address meeting elements that may not appear to be connected to spiritual formation. They are, however, essential to formational governance. In order for people to be open to God's forming activity, committees must work in the sort of open and collegial atmosphere addressed by these first questions. The remaining questions reflect essential elements for Christian formation in any setting. The answers you give to all of them will provide critical information about the way your congregation does business. They can lead you toward creating governance settings in which Christian formation and productive work both take place. In the paragraphs that follow, we will look at the elements revealed in the questions we've stated and explore the way their presence can affect our work together in the ministry of administration.

Listen

Is listening as a leadership skill emphasized among your members? Listening to one another is essential in any setting—but especially when decisions are being made. Good listening can lead to acceptance of one another's viewpoints as people work toward resolution in areas of conflict. Hearing one another clearly can avoid misunderstanding. Equipping church leadership teams with listening skills will enhance their effectiveness, and prepare them to listen to one another. Listening to one another, they may hear God's voice as well.

Be Informed

Are all members well-informed about the business of the committees with which they work? Very often, committee and council members begin work without any real understanding of the function of their group. I remember a time when my husband was a member of the trustees in a small congregation. The physical plant was their full responsibility. The men in this group spent two or three Saturdays each month at the church property. They installed and changed out lights, took care of the lawns, and replaced trash receptacles. The trustees had a good time doing this work and labored enthusiastically.

We later moved to a large downtown church. There the trustee responsibility was to administer funds held in trust. My husband was nominated and elected to the trustees because of his previous trustee experience. There was no briefing or job description available for new leaders. He was shocked at the first meeting to discover that this trustee board focused upon interest rates and investments! Their responsibility was the stewarding of the church's extensive trust funds. My husband had no experience and little interest, and was an ineffective trustee in that situation. Later, he was asked to serve on the Buildings and Grounds committee and contributed to that effort with great joy. I learned a good lesson from his experience. In order for people to be empowered to give their best efforts, they must know what is being expected of them! That is true for every member who serves in any capacity.

When everyone is well-informed about what is expected of them, people are more likely to be ready to participate meaningfully! When people are uninformed about issues and responsibilities and unprepared to listen to one another, discord and arguing are more likely to occur. On the other hand, a well-informed committee, prepared to listen to and for one another, is a group whose work is more likely to be fruitful. It will also be formational in a positive way.

Search the Scriptures

Is our work together grounded in Scripture? Is an opportunity to search the Scriptures together included in every meeting plan and agenda? If church leaders are regular in attendance at worship, they are hearing the Word read and preached each week. If they are, in addition, part of some continuing educational setting where Scripture reading and reflection take place, their participation is grounded in searching the Scripture. Experience has shown that not every church leader or committee member is in worship every week. Many are not in any continuing study. In order for our work to be grounded in the Word, we must allocate a generous portion of our meeting time for reflection on Scripture in the context of our work.

There are many ways to give leadership the opportunity for Scripture encounter, both privately and in the governance setting. In some congregations, the council or committee chair sends suggested Scripture reading and reflection along with the agenda for each monthly meeting. Every committee chair can be reflecting on passages that fellow leaders will study.

Ideally, every meeting of every committee or task force will begin with members searching the Scriptures together. A finance or stewardship committee might spend time with Jesus' words about money and the use of material wealth. An education committee might study Jesus' use of stories or reflect together on a parable. Perhaps all committees could work with the Lectionary selections for a particular week or season. However they encounter Scripture, leaders need to make reflection together a regular part of their work.

Pray

Is every meeting begun and continued in prayer? Are there people outside the meeting praying while it is in session? Do all committee members have the opportunity to pray for one another, and the congregation, between meetings? These three questions address perhaps the most important element in Christian spiritual formation and the most important support a congregation can give its leadership. Prayer is conversation with God, listening as well as talking. In administrative settings, prayer will "set the tone." When a meeting begins in conversation with God, God will be part of the conversation for the entire session. Invite church members in general to pray for committee meetings. This invitation will involve others in the work of administration as well as bring support through prayer.

Spiritual Leadership

Art Mills is in his fifth year as pastor of the Presbyterian Stone Church in Willow Glen in San Jose, California. He sees governing groups as a vital element in the spiritual formation of a congregation. "It is here," he says, "that the three-way relationship between self-God-other is lived out in important ways. The fragile and sacred relationship between individuals and God, and between one another, is tested in the throes of governance in the church."

Art's statement is the outgrowth of his own experience of ministry. Kevin's experience in the ministry of administration is an example of this "fragile and sacred relationship" in another congregation. Kevin became chairperson of his church's administrative council during a time of stress in the congregation. The church is in a changing neighborhood, and there were differences among its people about ways to be in ministry there. The congregation had recently undergone a pastoral change that some people were having a hard time accepting. In addition there were conflicts among the large staff that "bled" into the congregation.

Kevin began to consider his role during what would be a two-year term. He became convinced that a corporate spiritual practice was essential in the governing council. He believed the council meetings were a place where discipleship could be nurtured. Kevin set about planning meeting agendas which would create room for God to move and work as the council went about its business. A second goal was to instill the discipline and obedience to God that grows disciples. After some conversation with friends in other congregations, Kevin decided two elements were necessary for the success of his plan. First, he would keep Scripture in front of the group as they began their work at each meeting. He would encourage council members to consciously seek guidance from their Scripture reflection as meetings continued.

Second, celebration and prayer would be part of the agenda of every council meeting. Sessions would begin with both corporate and silent prayer. An important item on the agenda each month would be celebration in prayer of goals reached and new goals established. Members would be assigned a prayer partner to pray with and for between meetings. Most of the leadership group entered into Kevin's plans with enthusiasm. They were regular in attendance at worship and other activities and had also been looking for ways to ease the tension in the congregation.

Not everyone welcomed Kevin's plan. Several members of the council were not happy with his "waste" of meeting time. They let Kevin know that the time spent in Bible study and prayer got in the way of the "real" business of the council. These were capable people who had been chosen for leadership positions in order to encourage more active participation in the church life. They performed their tasks adequately but seldom attended the council meetings and were in worship only sporadically. In the meetings they did attend, they were generally a source of contention. They used the council sessions to vent their anger over conditions in the congregation.

As Kevin's first year as chair wore on, members attending the council meetings professed experiencing a growing sense of partnership as members of the body of Christ. They proposed other ways to be more active in prayer. One member suggested that they take the church directory and break up the list of family units so that each leader had a portion of the congregation. They began to pray for families each week. Some committee chairs broke up their lists among their committees as well, so that each of them shared in praying for the families of the congregation.

At the beginning of the second year, one of the nonparticipant leaders resigned and left the church. Others began to take part in the administrative council meetings more frequently. Council members were weathering this storm in their congregation and working together to ease the situation for church members. They began to feel that the experience of their meetings was helping them to be fruitful in ministry even in the face of an extremely difficult situation. They heard from church members that their prayers for the congregation were felt and appreciated. Instead of being defeated by a troubled time, these people were growing spiritually. They were being shaped by their attention to prayer and Scripture study together, as Kevin had hoped.

When his term was at an end, another member of the council was asked to serve as chair for the next two years. She agreed, and has continued the patterns Kevin initiated. Membership of the council has changed somewhat, and there is a new pastor. Conflict in the staff has ceased with several other changes. The administrative council's habits of work have remained in place although the "hard times" seem to be in the past. Governance in this congregation continues to develop as a setting for Christian formation.

New Models

In churches across the denominations, there are groups trying out new ways of governance and administration. For example, consider the possibility of a spiritual life committee. They begin their work year with a retreat, taking the opportunity to pay attention to their own spiritual lives before planning for the congregation. By the close of their retreat time, the group covenants to pray for one another and the church weekly, to search the Scriptures daily, and to participate in Holy Communion each week. They also agree to apply their creativity and energy into creating opportunities that encourage others in the congregation to practice the means of grace.

Having agreed to support one another's efforts to strengthen the spiritual life of the congregation, the group meets often in prayer or study or for retreat. They complete a survey of the ways the means of grace are presently practiced among church members. The members of the spiritual life committee are encouraged to enrich the spiritual life of the congregation as they feel led. The committee as a whole is using its considerable combined energy to support individual offerings of the members. They meet for business only rarely. It is an unusual way to operate, and might not prove workable at another time. This group, of course, does not exist. It is only my dream for what a spiritual life committee could be. It is possible!

Many church administrative groups are moving away from making decisions by votes to using a discernment model that seeks consensus. Instead of one "side" in any issue trying to convince the other, the community practices prayer, fasting, worship, and Christian conferencing as they listen for the Spirit's prompting. After corporate and silent prayer and a search in the Scriptures together, group members wait in silence until one person is moved to speak. They continue in discussion until all are in agreement. Often, decision making is preceded by a common fast ending with communion and a meal together. Learning to make decisions through discernment is not easy, but it is worth the effort.

A Vision for Administrative Groups

Every committee in every congregation can be a place of formation, a place of listening to one another and God. Ideally, leadership in every congregation might begin every new administrative year with a twelve- to twenty-four-hour retreat. At this retreat prayer, Scripture study, and worship would be the priority. Out of their study and prayer would flow vision and goals for the coming year. The work of filling the calendar with programs would take place in regular meetings.

During the year that followed, every meeting of every committee would begin with Scripture reflection and prayer. Every leader in the congregation would be invited to become a prayer partner with another person not in a leadership role. Primary leadership for our congregations might be chosen from among people who tithe regularly, are known to have an active prayer life, and participate in worship weekly. Might our ministry of governance be carried out differently if we did these things? Of course it would!

We would still be concerned with good communication, efficiency, and balanced budgets. But these methods of good governance would be lived out within the context of response to God's leading. Working in that context, every committee in every congregation would grow in grace. We would continue to recognize as we work that we are the body of Christ, serving in Christ's name. What a powerful blessing the church might be to the communities around us!

Administrative groups can be places of Christian formation when we remember that:
- administration is ministry, enabling the work of day-to-day ministry in Christ's name.
- the business of the church is carried out in response to God's grace in our lives.
- the context for this ministry is established through prayer and attention to the Word.

To help your particular administrative setting become a place of Christian formation, ask:
- Are we working carefully at listening to one another—do we know how to listen?
- Are all the members of the group kept informed of issues and plans involved in our work?
- Is there an opportunity to search the Scriptures together in every meeting of the group?
- Are meetings begun and continued in prayer?
- Are we celebrating and giving thanks for the product of our work?

Chapter Seven

Fellowship and Support Groups

Day by day, as they spent much time together . . .
they broke bread . . . and ate their food with glad
and generous hearts, praising God.

Acts 2:46-47

We were gathered for evening vespers. This was Friday evening of a four-day Christian educators' gathering that had begun the day before. It was Hettie's turn to lead, and she stood in front of our small group with origami paper and a pair of child's scissors in her hand. For the next five minutes or so, she spoke about her feelings for this twice-a-year gathering of friends. Hettie talked of her ministry being enriched by the fellowship she found here. She mentioned the support we had offered through the highs and lows of her changing marriage. As she talked, Hettie cut and folded almost automatically.

Finally, Hettie gave thanks to God for this circle of fellowship and support. Then she held up the circle of figures she had made as she talked. "Here you all are," she said, "a circle of friends. In the center is God." She had said better than any one of us could what it was that caused us to leave work and family and travel to spend this time together. This circle of friendship with God at its center was a cherished part of our lives.

From New Testament times, Christians have gathered for fellowship and in support of one another. There are also groups formed for other primary purposes where fellowship and support grow. The Christian educators' gathering is an example. In this chapter we will look at fellowship and support groups in the church today. These two kinds of groups often appear to be very much the same. The line between fellowship and support groups is sometimes fine. Sometimes it seems to disappear. But the primary purposes of fellowship and support groups differ.

Fellowship Groups

The purpose of the fellowship group is Christian social contact. It provides a setting for companionship among people of like beliefs and lifestyle. A church might establish a fellowship group for single adults of a particular age group or perhaps a fellowship of retired people. Youth fellowships exist in practically every congregation. Being part of any church fellowship group can lead to long-standing Christian friendships.

The fellowship group exists primarily for social interaction, and a major portion of the group's energy is put into planning and carrying out social activities. That social activity may be coffees or lunches after church. It may be evening gatherings that begin with a meal and sometimes include games and other programs. Whatever else the fellowship group is doing, the opportunity for Christian social interaction is at its center.

Support Groups

In a support group, the primary purpose is a community of support among people at a similar place in life or in a particular set of circumstances. A major function of the support group is the ministry of presence. Members listen to one another's stories. They comfort and strengthen one another by sharing their experience and learning. Many churches form support groups for recent widows or widowers, for young mothers, or for people living with diseases like cancer. There are support groups for recently divorced people and for single parents.

Years ago, I heard from an anthropologist friend that no group which remains focused strictly upon itself and its own well-being can continue to thrive. Time and experience have proven that saying true. Of course every group has a beginning and end and a natural life span. When groups remain centered solely on support for or fellowship among members, the life span will probably be very short.

Fellowship and support groups can become powerful settings for Christian formation without losing their essential purpose. Fellowship and support groups that incorporate the means of grace into their corporate lives will enrich both the lives of their members and the life of the community around them.

Moms on the Move

I know of a young mothers' support group that became a place of spiritual formation. Eventually that group enhanced the life of their congregation. One reason for their success was the creativity and energy of the members. Another is that from the beginning they practiced means of grace together.

"Moms on the Move," as they came to call themselves, began as a group of young women who had left the workplace to stay at home following the birth of their first children. Like many first-time mothers who have been successful in the world of work, some of the women expressed feelings of isolation and purposelessness. This was true even though all of them had waited eagerly for children and welcomed their sons or daughters. They expressed a need for support in their new way of life, and Moms on the Move ("MOMs") was born.

They met in one another's homes at midweek, sharing coffee and seasonal goodies. Their children were infants and came with their mothers to the meetings to be admired and cuddled by everyone. The moms also brought their Bibles. For the first half hour or so they explored Scripture, using the gospel or epistle readings from the lectionary. A brief conversation followed, centered on the places where the Scripture had touched their lives that week as comfort, confrontation, or challenge. They prayed together, giving thanks for God being at work in them. The rest of the morning was given over to general conversation, often focusing on whatever concern one of them might bring. As they talked, they often shared a craft one of them had tried. The hot glue gun was a constant companion! They ended the morning with a circle of quiet and a spoken benediction.

After the first few weeks the general conversation often turned to talk about concerns in the community around them. Many times the rest of the morning was spent at work on some project to benefit others less fortunate. For several weeks, the group planned ways to welcome newcomers with young children to the congregation.

When MOMs had been together almost two years, they learned of a need in the community that it would take substantial funds and assistance over time to meet. The group spent several mornings in conversation and prayer about their calling to meet this community need in Christ's name. They decided to take on the task as a group. Then they went to work and organized and produced a congregational cookbook to raise the money they would need.

These young women applied the same energy and creativity that had made them successful in the world of work to their lives as Christian parents. They made a difference in their families, in their congregation, and in the world around them. As they worked and prayed and supported one another, God was working in their lives, shaping them as a group and as individuals.

One of the original MOMs, Judy remembers this to be the time when she began to make friends in the church and become more involved with people outside her marriage. "It helped to be with others in my situation, and share our ups and downs. It was good to have some time for myself, in a Christian setting," she says.

As years passed and their children grew to school age, several of the women went back to work. Others moved away, and in time the group came to a natural end. The women remained friends in Christ. Being part of Moms on the Move had been an important part of the lives of its members. This support group with Christ at its center formed their spirits—and their lives— at a crucial time. The members had become women of strong faith.

The L.A.W. Bunch

The L.A.W. Bunch began as eight or nine singles at a large church who went for Lunch After Worship each Sunday. Their sole purpose was a kind of fellowship not available on the local "singles scene" in their city. After a few weeks, the original group started using the church bulletin to let others know they would be welcome.

The group grew quickly. Over lunch they often discussed the morning's sermon or the various Sunday school classes they attended. Conversation often turned to events in their lives that week or the city's professional basketball team. The lunch hour sometimes extended to a pick-up ball game or swimming at one apartment complex or another. They learned about one another's professional and personal lives—and the concerns they shared.

The L.A.W. Bunch enjoyed being together. After some months, however, they began to feel that something was missing in their group. They weren't sure what that "something" was. At about the same time, missionaries on home leave from their station in Belize visited the congregation. In their presentation, they talked about the recent devastation caused by a hurricane. At lunch that Sunday, the L.A.W. Bunch talked about the missionaries and the damage in Belize. "There must be things we can do to help," was their consensus. They ended their lunch with prayer for the missionaries and the people they served. They commissioned one of the group members to talk to someone on the church staff about Belize that week.

After conversations with church staff, the L.A.W. Bunch "rep" proposed a work trip to Belize. Members who could get time away from work would fly down and rebuild a chapel and perhaps a house at the mission station.

They planned to stay in the dorm at the school there. Those who couldn't get time off to go on the trip would support it with money and prayer.

With help from their church staff the trip was organized. Eleven L.A.W. Bunch folks traveled to Belize. All agreed it was the best experience of their lives. They returned with stories both hilarious and hair-raising. They also brought back exotic fruits for everyone along with their sunburned faces and sun-bleached hair and many photographs. As weeks passed it became obvious to their friends that the travelers had brought back a renewed and strengthened relationship to God as well.

For those who traveled and those who gave support from home, the mission trip to Belize had been a great success. Soon, plans were underway for a return trip the next year. Everyone who could arranged to have time off to go. As they met for lunch on Sundays, and in twos or threes informally at other times during the week, the members of the L.A.W. Bunch were often in prayer for the mission in Belize.

Over the years that followed, the L.A.W. Bunch made several work trips to Central and South America. In their service to others they worked long hours and enjoyed themselves outrageously. They learned about a culture very different from their own. They formed lasting friendship bonds within their own group and with the people they went to serve. Several men and women discovered life mates in the group during their mission adventures. In carrying the grace of God to people in need, the L.A.W. Bunch found new awareness of God's love, mercy, and grace in their own lives.

The Lunch After Worship Bunch may not be typical of fellowship groups. They are, however, an example of what can happen when groups let themselves be open to leading from God. They began as a group of committed Christians searching for friendships among persons who shared their beliefs. They have become a group of men and women growing in relationship to God through their experience of service to others. Sharing in this means of grace has altered and widened their lives.

Fellowship groups can become places of formation when leaders intentionally incorporate means of grace into group life. They need not lose their spontaneous fun and rich friendships in the process! Changes to the group pattern may be as simple as adding an informal grace at meals and closing with a time of prayer. If your group is already doing these things, you may want to add opportunities for service to others. It is important to retain the character of your group, not making service the primary focus but making it one part of the fellowship life of the group.

The "Super Adults"

In one congregation, there is a group for older adults called Super Adults. Many congregations have a similar type of group. At Super Adults, the focus is on fellowship among the retired people who belong to the group. They have game days and book review days. They take day trips in the area and often sponsor longer tours. They eat lunch at the church one day a month and hear an informative or entertaining program. All these things are done in an atmosphere of Christian caring and fellowship.

Super Adults is keeping its older members from isolation and loneliness. It is also doing more. The support committee has set up a "keep in touch" network, making daily phone calls to members who cannot leave their homes to check on their well-being. Other committee members provide rides to doctor's appointments or do grocery shopping. Books to read or listen to are available from the Super Adult lending library.

In addition to worshiping together and praying for one another, Super Adults give service to one another and to the church community. They are invaluable helpers in the vacation Bible school and other outreach efforts in the neighborhood. On a recent Saturday they sponsored a Labyrinth prayer experience for the whole congregation. They are continuing, through the means of grace, to grow in faith as they grow in years.

Fellowship, Support, and Christian Formation

Whether groups are organized by professional staff or interested lay-people, they can become places of Christian formation. One key is to make one or more of the means of grace part of the corporate life of the group. Another is to maintain the essential purpose of the group.

When beginning new groups, make prayer for one another, the group, and the community part of your meeting pattern. Gently encourage conversation around the faith journeys of members as opportunities arise.

As the support or fellowship group continues, challenge members to join in service to others in Christ's name. Very often service will arise naturally out of the interests and concerns in the group. A cancer support group might begin work with one of the agencies doing education and prevention activities in many cities. A fellowship of senior adults could decide to do "grandma and grandpa duty" in the rocking chair of the church childcare center. There are many, varied possibilities available. Sharing the love of God with others will help members to be aware of that love in their own circumstances.

Changing the operating mode of an already existing group can be a challenge. One way to begin is to make your own informal inventory of the group's ongoing agenda. Perhaps Christian formation is already happening there. Questions you might ask yourself include these: If you share a meal, is there always prayer before or after? Do you end your gatherings with prayer and a benediction of some sort? Is there a ministry of presence in the group—do members share their joys and concerns informally? Do they share their faith stories in support of one another? Is there a fairly consistent pattern of concern for people outside the group and a response to perceived needs? Is there ever any conversation centered around Scripture or opportunity for response to Scripture in the context of one's life experience? If you can answer yes to three or even two of these questions about your group, there is no need for any huge changes!

If the group has a pattern of accepting all persons, and if there is clear communication and a feeling of safety for members, you are in a good place. You are already providing an atmosphere in which God will work to form persons as Christian disciples. Give thanks!

If you cannot answer yes to any of these questions, begin to pray for the group. As you open to God with this need, you will begin to notice small ways you can help your group to add the means of grace to your corporate life. Remember always that the essential character of your group is support in a life situation or Christian fellowship. Perhaps you might suggest that your group begin lunch or supper with singing grace. Perhaps you might raise a concern and ask for prayer in conversation. It is not always easy to be the one who says, "I feel the need of a prayer circle of support before we go." But that circle will add to the richness of your fellowship. Someone may say to you later, "Thanks, I needed that!"

The process of Christian formation is always continuing, just as the need for fellowship and support in life situations is with us always. Every Christian setting for support and/or fellowship can also be a "Traveler's Aid" station on the journey of formation as Christian disciples.

Fellowship and support groups can be powerful settings for Christian spiritual formation. It is important in the process of becoming more formational not to lose sight of the original purpose of the group. Retaining the essential quality of the group, you can "mix in" various means of grace. When you do, your fellowship or support group becomes much more—a place where Christian disciples can grow.

Enhance spiritual formation in your fellowship group by:
- making prayer for your group a priority in your own life.
- participating in service to others as a group and reflecting on the experience.
- making prayer part of your regular meetings.
- discussing one another's faith stories from time to time.
- adding more participation in the means of grace. If you are concerned about your group, make a small informal inventory, then introduce one of the means of grace gently and quietly. Perhaps it will be grace before meals or a circle of intercession at your close.

Chapter Eight

Leading a Group

Unless the LORD builds the house,
  those who build it labor in vain.
Unless the LORD guards the city,
  the guard keeps watch in vain.

Psalm 127:1

hristian formation is a journey that is never complete. We are by grace always moving toward the holiness God intends for each of us. My favorite symbol for this process is the Slinky toy. The Slinky is a continuous spiral of metal or plastic wire that freely stretches or contracts. When encouraged with a gentle pull or push, it moves off in new directions. It is seldom still unless put up in its box. The process of Christian spiritual formation is a continuous spiral that can resemble the Slinky. In that process the human spirit is sometimes stretched to new limits. Sometimes it contracts to reflect. Always it is in the process of being renewed. There are differences between us and the Slinky—of course! One great difference is that as humans we can sometimes control the Slinky toy. Yet we can seldom control the ways in which our human spirits are shaped by every event and each person we encounter. When we are open to God, it is God who shapes us, in love and grace.

Our world needs desperately to know that love and grace today. In every community there are scores of people searching for meaning in their lives through hurried activity or long hours of work. Others attempt to lose themselves in dangerous substances or mind-numbing television and films. Countless others seek to become "good enough" to be loved by God, struggling apart from any community support. We are called to reach out to these people in every Christian congregation. They are longing to begin the journey of return to the God who creates us. They just don't know how.

In Christian settings, we can help people looking for God to find community. This need for spiritual community is as great as it has been at any time. The church can be a starting place for new life for every hungering person. We can offer to everyone an example of the grace and love of God. This means that every meeting, every class, every gathering in our congregations must be a setting that offers opportunity for positive Christian formation. Our meetings must reflect God and not the business practices and habits of the world around us.

The primary goal of this book is to help you discover that you can plan meetings in which participants are helped to be open to God and to the process of Christian spiritual formation. Another goal is to provide methods and tools for accomplishing that end. It has been fun for me to tell stories about the ways people become open to being shaped by God. It is exciting to relate the process by which a small group affects the growing faith experience of its members. It is relatively simple to talk and write about making Christian formation a part of every meeting of every group in the congregation.

Creating a setting in which Christian faith formation can happen month after month is another matter altogether! It requires consistent effort to accomplish. How do we go about creating such a setting? What are the resources we need? Where do we begin? The answer to that last question is to start with yourself. The place for you—the group leader or teacher or chairperson—to begin is with your own growing relationship to God in Jesus Christ. Your own growing faith is the most important resource you possess as you work in the church. It is also the most important ingredient in making any meeting you lead a place of Christian formation. As your relationship to God deepens, you will become constantly more aware of God's presence. You will be more ready to listen for God's leading and to follow.

I do not mean to imply that only the "spiritually mature" should be chosen as leaders in congregations. Any person possessing gifts for leadership must be given the opportunity to develop and use those gifts within the community of faith. What I am saying is that as a leader, part of your responsibility is to continue to grow in faith and in relationship to God. Your style of leadership will develop along with that relationship.

Your growing faith will be nourished as you develop holy habits—attendance at worship, reading Scripture in some regular way, and daily prayer. Your faith will be nurtured in a Sunday school class or other intentional small-group setting and by conversation with others about your experience of God's mercy and grace. Making those means of grace part of your daily life will help you to be open to God's work in you—to your own Christian formation. You are to work at your own faith as you plan strategies to make your committee or other group a place where faith can grow in all the participants!

The Next Step

After your own living Christian faith, the next important ingredient in creating the formational group setting is a published agenda that establishes a place and time for prayer and searching the Scriptures together. To see how this might work, let's visit Amy Lee as she prepares for a meeting of the education committee. Amy's interest in religious education rises out of her own trials as a single parent trying to raise her children to be faithful Christians. In a crowded life, Amy has to work at finding time for her own spiritual growth. She uses the hour riding the commuter train into her city job each day to read her Bible and pray. As her quarterly education committee meeting approaches, Amy keeps their work in mind during her reading and prayer each morning. The committee will be talking about summer Sunday school and vacation Bible school at the coming meeting. As she reads one morning, Amy is struck by Jesus' words to his disciples: "Let the little children come to me, and do not stop them." She wonders, "'What are we doing that may hinder children from coming closer to Christ in our learning settings? What are we not doing that may hinder our adult workers from coming closer to Christ in their leadership experience?"

Her purpose for the next education committee meeting becomes clear in Amy's mind. She would like the children to feel openness to God in all their sessions of summer Sunday school and VBS. She will ask her committee to make this the goal of their planning. She will be praying for all the committee, that God will make clear to them what they need to do.

Amy reflects on the Scripture and her questions and goals off and on for several days. Then one night after her children are asleep, she works on a letter to remind committee members of their coming meeting and announce the agenda. The letter she composes looks like this:

Dear Friends,

Our quarterly meeting is approaching. I am writing to remind you that we will meet in the library at 5:30 PM on Wednesday, March 4. Please pick up your meal in the supper line and be ready to go to work as we eat!

In my own study, I have been reading in Matthew this week. Matthew 19:13-15 was quite striking to me as I considered our education ministry with children. In my translation, verse 14 reads, "Jesus said, 'Let the little children come to me, and do not stop them.' " It seemed to me that this verse is an appropriate passage to consider as we prepare and pray for our planning meeting. Wouldn't it be wonderful if our children could encounter an atmosphere that encourages their openness to God in all our education settings this summer? I hope you will join me in prayer that our work will have that result! I have enclosed a copy of our agenda to help you get ready for this important session.

I hope that you are as eager as I am to continue the plans we began for our children this summer and that you will be full of ideas when we meet. Please continue to pray for our children, their parents, our teachers, and our education committee work.

Your sister in Christ,

Amy Lee

Agenda, Education Committee Meeting

Opening Prayer

"Time Out" with Scripture—my questions around Matthew chapter 19:13-15 include this one: How might we as Christian educators be hindering our children from coming closer to Jesus in our Sunday school? What can we do to improve?

Continuing Business: Summer Sunday School: Theme, Ideal Leaders, Time Frames, Recruitment, Curriculum materials

Vacation Bible School—Where will we find room for more children? How can we better assist our VBS Director in her work? Is it too early to order materials and begin to recruit?

Creating an atmosphere in which children can be open to God—How do we start? What about personnel and training? What can I do to encourage this?

New Business: Bibles for third graders—June or September?

Concerns of Committee Members

Celebration, Prayer, and Praise to send us out

Amy has done at least two things with this letter. First, she has let everyone know her own primary goals for the summer programs and the questions raised in her mind by Scripture. Second, she has told her committee members that she is preparing beforehand for their meeting and expects them to do the same. With the agenda, she has shown them, as she does for each meeting, that searching the Scripture and reflecting together is important to her. She has given those few moments priority in her planning. She has also laid out clearly her intentions for the meeting and has allowed time for concerns the members bring. They will come to the meeting knowing that their ideas and concerns will be heard and respected.

Every letter may not be as enthusiastic as Amy's. Others will be more businesslike. However, each one can have the same strong influence with committee members. Your letter should be clear and concise. It should spell out the business you will be addressing and your goals. It should include Scripture you have encountered that you feel illuminates the work of the group. It should encourage members to reflect with Scripture and to pray for the meeting.

Choosing Scripture

Choosing Scripture for reflection is a personal thing, for the Bible touches each of us in different ways. Many people choose to read the daily lectionary passages in their devotional reading. Others use the guidance of some devotional book. Both are useful paths. If in your daily reading you encounter Scripture that has meaning for you in terms of the small group you are leading, that passage would be your first choice to share with group members and to use in reflection as you prepare.

If you do not encounter a passage that speaks to your ministry role, you might want to choose a "topical" passage. However you choose the Scripture for your meeting context, it is important to spend time with it, to let the words speak to your concerns for your group.

Why Share Scripture With the Group?

There is one primary reason for encouraging your group members to encounter Scripture as part of their preparation for meeting times. Reading Scripture as a group gives your work a clear context of faith. It is easy to neglect the "why" of our labors in the church as we become bogged down in the "who, what, when, and where" of ministry. Encountering and reflecting upon Scripture as a group will bring us back to the reasons for our work. We are, after all, serving God in Jesus Christ in all we do. In addition, Scripture reflection will encourage your group's openness to God's leading as they prepare.

For the same reasons, you will want participants to be in prayer for your meetings. Their prayer will result in an expectancy and awareness of God's guiding presence as you meet. Members will be open to God's leading and be ready to follow.

Let Scripture Inspire Your Work

The "Merry Men" is a group of retirees who get together on Thursday mornings to do chores around the church. They meet in the kitchen for donuts and coffee at 9:00 AM, then make a plan for the day and act on it. Just now they are putting in many hours of "overtime" readying the flower beds and grass around our main entrance for Spring. They have tilled and planted and fed the plants and grass. By Easter the approach to the Sanctuary will be lovely—a riot of color. Their inspiration has come from the Psalms: "Enter his gates with thanksgiving, and his courts with praise" (Psalm 100:4a). Their intent is to create a setting that will lift people's hearts to praise as they enter the church.

In whatever work you do in your congregation, Scripture can inspire you. Let the ancient witness to God's work in the world speak to your committee or task force in every meeting. Listen to what your members hear in Scripture and give them the opportunity to share their inspiration with the whole group. You will find your meetings—and your work as a whole—enriched.

Moving On

When your agenda is set and members have been notified of a meeting, when you have taken time to reflect and pray, it is time to move on to the meeting itself. This might be a good time to talk about the necessity of keeping that meeting moving. There is a fine line between giving everyone room and time to speak—and letting meetings drag out into needless repetition that often leads to nonproductive wrangling! It is sometimes a good thing to let your watchword for meeting times be "Keep it moving!"

A complete agenda, which everyone has in advance, will help with this endeavor. If, when you distribute an agenda, one or two members call with large concerns to address, it is an easy matter to discuss whether or not they might be included and make a decision. In the meeting, it is important to be ready to say, when potentially lengthy issues arise during "concerns of the members," that the issue deserves more time than is available now and will be taken up at the next meeting.

It is important to do what you advertise doing in a meeting and then stop. An old friend of mine says often that there is nothing that really needs doing that cannot be accomplished in a meeting of two hours or less. She prefers an hour and a half. I think she is right! After an hour, people begin to be tired and anxious to get to other things that need their attention. When people arrive well prepared, you can move rapidly and productively through an agenda. Then it is possible to dismiss before people have become exhausted and impatient.

It is also important to stick to your intent to begin and end with prayer and praise, with attention to Scripture, so that you create a context of faith to work within.

Making this a habit will create a setting in which people will be open to the moving of God in your meeting and in themselves. If you are uncertain about your skills for leading a meeting, look in your church or library for one of the several good "how-to" books for leaders. Or ask about your district leadership training or request training in leading a meeting from your congregation. Leading an efficient and productive meeting is a skill that is relatively easy to learn and that will assist you in the task of making your meeting setting a formational one.

What Comes Next?

So, you have conducted a meeting in which participants had the opportunity to reflect on Scripture and pray. They accomplished the items listed in their agenda. They dismissed with thanksgiving and praise. What remains for you to do? My recommendation is that, as soon after the meeting as you find time, you write or e-mail your group members once more. In this communication, you will want to review the accomplishments and decisions of the meeting and list what tasks were undertaken by each member. This letter can be both a gentle reminder and a celebration of your work. You may want to repeat the Scripture which inspired you as you prepared and to comment on how the group members have lived into that Scripture by their actions.

Your next step—and it is an essential one—is to see that decisions that you have made are being implemented. First, carry out the things for which you took responsibility, then make calls as the weeks go by to check out the ways in which committee members are working. Offer them your support and prayer and give thanks with them when they have completed tasks. Make sure that other church leaders are kept aware of the work of your committee and that pastor and staff are giving their support where it is needed.

Your committee members and those who interact with you will have an example of the church at work which is distinctly different from the example of the world around them. You will have a scriptural vision of the church at work, driven by mutual study and prayer. Your ministry in Christ's name will have implications for the church beyond your own committee. Through God's mercy, you will be an example in your congregation and in your community. All this is possible—you have only to pray and work and follow God's leading and it will happen. The satisfaction will be yours—and you will give glory to God.

As you prepare and lead a small group:
- Concentrate on your own deepening relationship to God.
- Keep open communication with fellow participants.
- Create a clear agenda for every meeting that makes room and time for prayer and reflection.
- Let Scripture set the context, inspire, and encourage.
- Do what you intend to do, then celebrate!
- Communicate after the meeting to remind and encourage.
- Call on the pastor and staff for support.
- If you are not confident of your skills, find ways to learn.
- Give thanks and glory to God!

Last Thoughts

The grace of the Lord Jesus be with you. My love be with all of you in Christ Jesus.

1 Corinthians 16:23-24

We celebrate the beginning of the Christmas season each year with a gathering of friends and family. As people arrived at our favorite breakfast restaurant last December, there was a lot of laughter and hugs and greetings all around. We stood in the light-filled room talking and laughing and generally "catching up" as the restaurant staff laid out a buffet.

After a little while I took hold of the hand of the person standing on each side, others followed suit, and we fell silent. Donna, our colleague and friend, gave thanks for the blessings of the year, for all of us gathered, and for the food. She asked God's blessing on all of us, on those absent whom we loved and on the workers preparing and serving our food. Together we all said "Amen," and the noisy celebration continued.

Long after the last biscuits and gravy and other "goodies" were eaten we lingered around the tables talking. Children ran and played in the room. When we stood to leave the exchanging of hugs and loving words took a long time. It was a joyful, beautiful morning.

That celebration showed me once more the incalculable value of Christian community. Looking around the room, I knew that those gathered could count on me for anything I could do or provide that they needed, at any time, without exception. I knew Tom and I could count on them. I knew that as I pray for them daily, they pray for us. And I knew that more than we love one another we love the God we worship and serve together.

We have sat in learning settings together. We have worked together in service to others. We have all worshiped together at one time or another and have let the Scriptures illumine our lives and our relationships to one another. We have prayed for one another in celebration and in sorrow. We have shared in the means of grace and have been shaped by God into the people we are today.

A dozen of the folks at the celebration were our children and grandchildren. The companions of our Emmaus reunion groups were there. People with whom we have served on mission work teams joined us. Some were contemporaries we have known in Sunday school. All of us have been formed by our common experience and by our relationships one with another into the Christian disciples we are today. All of us have been blessed richly, so that we might bless the lives of others in Christ's name.

In the midst of this company on a morning in early December, I was poignantly aware of the work that God is doing in all God's children. That work goes on within communities of folks who meet for whatever purpose, at whatever time in Christ's name. The heart's journey never ends. God's work in each of us continues. In time we come to a place where we can truly say we work and play and praise in the name and for the sake of the One who creates and redeems us. That is the priceless gift of Christian formation, which can be at the heart of the life of every Christian small group. Thanks be to God!

Suggested Resources

In spiritual formation, as in any other undertaking, the key is to find the resource that best suits your situation and use it!

Alive Now, a bimonthly publication of the Upper Room. This small magazine contains reading for reflection along with questions for discussion and accompanying Scripture readings. An excellent resource for serving or administrative groups.

As If the Heart Mattered: A Wesleyan Spirituality, by Gregory S. Clapper (Upper Room, 1997). This Pathways in Spiritual Growth book is an introduction to Wesleyan spirituality and the means of grace.

Bread for the Journey: A Daybook of Wisdom and Faith, by Henri J. M. Nouwen (HarperSanFrancisco, 1997).

The Cup of Our Life: A Guide for Spiritual Growth, by Joyce Rupp (Ave Maria Press, 1997). This is a great resource for a continuing group and can be used fruitfully by men and women alike.

Devotional Classics: Selected Readings for Individuals and Groups, edited by Richard J. Foster and James Bryan Smith (HarperSanFrancisco, 1993).

Devotional Life in the Wesleyan Tradition, by Steve Harper (Upper Room, 1983). A study of Wesley's use of the means of grace in a disciplined devotional life.

A Diary of Private Prayer, by John Baillie (Scribners, 1949). A classic guide with space for your own reflections.

A Guide to Prayer for All God's People, collected and edited by Rueben P. Job and Norman Shawchuck (Upper Room, 1990). A classic daily devotional guide.

Keeping in Touch: Christian Formation and Teaching, by Carol F. Krau (Discipleship Resources, 1999). A splendid resource for every teacher and leader in education ministry.

The Practice of the Presence of God, by Brother Lawrence, translated by Robert J. Edmonson (Paraclete Press, 1984). Part of the Christian Classics series.

Prayer and Our Bodies, by Flora Slosson Wuellner (Upper Room, 1987). An excellent personal or group resource.

Praying With Julian of Norwich, by Gloria Durka (St. Mary's Press, 1995). This small book is part of the series Companions for the Journey. Others in the series include St. Benedict, Francis of Assisi, Ignatius of Loyola, Teresa of Avila, and Thomas Merton.

The Spiritual Formation Bible: Growing in Intimacy With God Through Scripture, developed by The Upper Room and published by Zondervan, 1999. Published in both hardcover and paperback.